Hindus and Tribals

— Quest for a Co-Existence —

Hindus and Tribals

— Quest for a Co-Existence —
(Social Dynamics in Medieval Orissa)

Gaganendra Nath Dash

Decent Books

New Delhi

Published by
Decent Books
D-36/A-1, Mohan Garden
New Delhi - 110 059

Distributed by
D. K. Printworld (P) Ltd.
'*Sri Kunj*', F-52, Bali Nagar
New Delhi - 110 015
Phones : (011) 545-3975; 546-6019

Printed by
DP's Impressive Impressions, New Delhi - 110 059

ISBN 81-86921-01-X

First Published in India: 1998

The publication of this book has been financially supported by the Indian Council of Historical Research. The responsibility for the facts stated or opinions expressed is entirely of the author and not of the ICHR.

For
Rama, Tapan
and
Pratichi

Preface

I

THIS small monograph is an extended version of a paper the first draft of which was prepared in later 1973 under the title, "The Role of the Priests in the Development of Indradyumna Legend". The type-script of this draft paper was circulated among the members of the Orissa Research Project sponsored by the South Asia Institute, University of Heidelberg, West Germany as a part of the Interdisciplinary Regional Research Programme (SFB 16) fully financed by the German Research Council (DFG), Bonn. The project with members drawn from different disciplines belonging to the universities of Heidelberg and Freiburg in West Germany, and University of Udayapur, Visva-Bharati and Utkal University in India was primarily studying the formation and function of the regional tradition as exemplified in the cult of Jagannatha in Orissa. I had the opportunity to work as a Member (and for some time as the Field Director) of this Project. The preparation of my draft paper can be said to be a direct outcome of another draft paper titled, "Ksatriyaization and Social Change: A Study in Orissa Setting", written and circulated among the members of the Project by Hermann Kulke, a member-colleague in the Project which has subsequently been published. Ruprecht Geib, another member-colleague, was also then engaged in studying the Indradyumna legend thoroughly in order to shed new light on the origin and development of the cult of Jagannatha, which might have been indirectly responsible for attracting my attention to the same traditional account. Later, some of my findings were incorporated in two of my papers on the Evolution of the Priestly Power which were included, along with 23 other papers written by the members of the Project, in the comprehensive volume *The Cult of Jagannatha and the Regional Tradition of Orissa* (1978) edited by A. Eschmann, H. Kulke and G.C. Tripathi in which most of the major findings of the Project have been published.

In 1979 a much revised and enlarged version of my original draft paper was presented in a seminar held in Bhubaneswar under the auspices of Centre for Advanced Study in History and Culture, Bhubaneswar. Both H. Kulke and Bhabagrahi Misra were shown this revised version and they in turn offered their comments. Still later a further enlarged Oriya version was prepared and published in the literary monthly, *The Jhankar* in 1981. Between 1984 and 1985 when I was working on a fellowship from the ICHR, New Delhi an improved and further enlarged version was prepared. When I visited Germany 1987-88 on a cultural exchange programme sponsored by the German Academic Exchange Service (DAAD), I carried the same with me. There, Prof. H. von Stietencron, Professor of Indology and Comparative Religion, University of Tuebingen and a former member-colleague in the Orissa Research Project was kind enough to go through this rather very long paper and agreed with most of my conclusions. This was a source of great encouragement to me. At Tuebingen I also got the opportunity to collect some more material on the subject at the excellent collection on India in the famous central library of the University of Tuebingen as well as in the Seminar Library of the Department of Indology. After I came back from Germany I decided to publish this already long paper in the form of a small book. The present monograph is the outcome of that decision.

After the manuscript of this monograph was prepared Hermann Kulke, my former colleague in Orissa Research Project and presently Professor, Chair of Asian History, Kiel University,

Germany went through the entire manuscript thoroughly and offered his comments while generally appreciating the work. Some of his comments were later utilized in revising the monograph. Among other things he suggested to me the term ksatriyaization which I decided to accept and use but for a different phenomenon. I am grateful to Hermann Kulke for his comments, suggestions and appreciation.

II

In this small monograph an attempt has been made to study the interaction of the socio-economic, religious, cultural forces and counter-forces unlike the traditional historical works in the field of Orissan historiography which generally address themselves to record primarily—if not exclusively—the political (and perhaps also the military) events with extensive care and excessive zeal subordinating everything else to that. This is a new trend in Orissan historiography and was almost completely unknown prior to conscious and pioneering attempts made in this direction by the members of erstwhile Orissa Research Project in their various publications. This new trend was based on the assumption that it is absolutely necessary to study the inter-play of the socio-economic and religious-cultural forces and counter-forces in order to be able to understand and reconstruct history as sometimes—if not invariably always—the political and even the military events are rooted in the same. In contrast, the earlier trend of recording primarily the political and military events subordinating everything else to that is based on the belief that the social, economic, religious and cultural events are not related to one another; they are subsidiary to the political and military events and perhaps also always sprang from the same source if not completely independent developments. The earlier trend had resulted in the production of a number of papers and books on Orissan history usually adopting a framework in which after political and military events were presented most prominently the social, economic, religious, educational, cultural and administrative (revenue and judiciary, etc.) events were grouped together, then arranged chronologically and finally presented in a manner as if these events were completely unrelated, independent developments if not — which is more likely — shown to be somehow rooted in political and military events. As opposed to that, the new trend in turn has set another methodological new trend of using the concepts and methodological tools of other social sciences, especially of ethnology, to analyse and understand the historical data. Though these two new trends created a stir among the scholars, especially the historians of Orissa specifically immediately after the publication of the earlier mentioned *The Cult of Jagannatha and the Regional Tradition of Orissa* in 1978, they have not been able to make much headway since then due to the adverse reaction of some scholars of traditional school with conservative outlook. The present monograph endeavours to take these new trends only a step forward. If it would be able to induce some future scholars to follow up these new trends I will consider myself amply rewarded.

III

Besides, this small monograph seeks to set two new trends in the Orissan historiography. Firstly in this work much more weightage has been given to the traditional account as a source material of history than is the practice in the contemporary Orissan scene. (Why and in what circumstances the importance of the traditional accounts as a source material of Orissan history has been minimized has been explained elsewhere in this work). Further, the traditional account has been subjected to a completely novel method of analysis here in order to extract the historical truth — flowing like an undercurrent — out of the same. It has been sought to discover the historical background of the emergence and evolution of the traditional account in contrast to seeking to dig out the historical basis of the same — if any — in order to arrive at the historical truth. That way this little monograph promises to be a trend-setter at least in the context of Orissan historiography

(Dr. Ruprect Geib's excellent work on Indradyumna legend though a pioneering work in the field is virtually unknown in Orissa as it is written in German). Of course since the late seventies I have been attaching much more importance to the traditional account as a source material of history and adopting this new method of analysing the same while reconstructing the socio-religious history of Orissa in my various papers and in my monograph titled, *Janasruti Kanci-Kaveri* (1979) written in Oriya. Though these have been able to attract the attention of the scholars and other intellectuals of Orissa in general to the importance of the traditional accounts as a source material and to the methodological innovation in analysing the same, the professional historians, i.e., those who teach history in colleges and universities being generally of conventional and conservative outlook have tended to ignore though not outrightly reject them. (Among only a few exceptions the name of Kailash Chandra Dash is worth mentioning who has shown active interest in them). I now very sincerely hope that this little monograph will be able to induce some young professional historians of Orissa to give the traditional accounts their due, which has been long denied to them as a source material of history and undertake and sharpen the new method employed here to analyse the same which will be a source of immense pleasure to me. With this end in view another unpublished paper of mine with the traditional accounts as the major source material has been given at the end as appendix.

Furthermore this monograph seeks to study the tribal absorption into the Hindu society and after that their upward movement in the hierarchy of the *jatis* in the medieval period at the micro level besides shedding some new light on the history of the cut of Jagannatha. And this phenomenon of tribal absorption-cum-jati mobility manifests a quest for co-existence on the part of Hindus on one hand and in Orissa played a pivotal role proving a common meeting ground. How far I have been successful in my attempt is for others to judge.

G.N. Dash

Acknowledgements

I AM indebted to the German Research Council, (DFG), Bonn and the authorities of the South Asia Interdisciplinary Regional Research Programme (SFB 16) at the South Asia Institute at the University of Heidelberg, Germany especially Prof. Dietmar Rothermund for giving me the opportunity to work as a member of the Orissa Research Project in the seventies which enabled me to undertake this work.

I am grateful to the University Grants Commission, New Delhi and the German Academic Exchange Service (DAAD), Bonn for enabling me to visit Germany in 1987-88 on a cultural exchange programme which provided me with the opportunities to collect more materials on the subject and discuss my findings with my German counterpart Prof. H. von Stietencron.

I am also grateful to the Indian Council of Historical Research, New Delhi for granting me a fellowship during the tenure of which I was able to prepare an earlier version of this monograph.

I express my deep gratitude to my colleagues in the Orissa Research Project: late Prof. U. Schneider, Prof. H. von Stietencron, Prof. H. Kulke, Prof. G. Pfeffer, Prof. J. Lütt Prof. G.G. Tripathi, Dr. R. Geib, late Dr. A. Eschmann, Dr. J. Rösel and Mr. E. Hein who unhesitatingly accepted me as a member-colleague and offered all sorts of cooperation and encouragement while I was working with them.

I am especially grateful to Prof. H. Kulke, Dr. Bhabagrahi Misra and Prof. H. von Stietencron who have kindly gone through earlier versions of this monograph and offered their comments.

I am thankful to Prof. K.C. Sahu for providing me with a paper-copy of a palm-leaf manuscript of Deula Tola by Magunia Das. I am also thankful to Sri Safalya Kumar Nandi and Sri Arun Kumar Das, of the National Library, Calcutta, who helped me to procure a xeroxed copy of Sri Ksetra Mahatmya ba Deula Tola by one Damu Das from the National Library.

Besides I am grateful to many others who have helped me either materially or otherwise in the preparation of this monograph. Although it is not possible to mention each individual by name here, I remember them with fond gratitude.

G.N. Dash

P.S. Some of my friends has referred this study as Tribal Priests of a Hindu shrine, in their writings. This was the title I assumed when the work was as the manuscript stage. I regret for this confusion.

The earlier title of this monograph was Tribal Priests of a Hindu Shrine. some of my friends who had seen the earlier pre-publication draft of this work have referred to this monograph by its former title in their writings. I am extremely sorry for this confusion.

It needs to be borne in mind that all references to the districts of Orissa in this work pertain to the pre-1993 undivided districts of the state.

Contents

Abbreviations

EI	*Epigraphia Indica*
JASB	*Journal of the Asiatic Society of Bengal*

1
Tribal Absorption and Jati Mobility

It is M.N. Srinivas who is generally credited with the first ever serious and systematic attempt to scientifically define and provide a comprehensive conceptual framework for the study of the complex process of tribal absorption-cum-*jati* mobility as early as 1952 in his subsequently famous work *The Religion and Society among the Coorgs of South India* though others had made observation of this complex phenomena even earlier.[1] He gave the label 'Sanskritization' to this complex process of tribal absorption into the Hindu society and the mobility of the *jatis* in the *varna* scale.[2] He described this complex process in the following manner.

> The idea of caste as a five-fold division of society represents a gross simplification of facts. The real unit of caste system is not one of the five varnas, but jati, which is very small endogamous group practising a traditonal occupation and enjoying a certain amount of cultural, ritual, and juridical autonomy . . . . The importance of varna-system consists that it furnishes an All-India frame into which the myriad jatis in any single linguistic area can be fitted. It systematizes the chaos of jatis and enables the sub-caste of one region to be comprehended by people in another area by reference to a common scale. Further, the varna-system represents a scale of values, and jatis occupying the lower rungs have throughout

> tried to raise their status by taking over the customs and rituals of the top jatis.[3]

Srinivas further observed,

> The caste system is far from a rigid system in which the position of each component caste is fixed for all time. Movement has always been possible, and especially so in the middle regions of the hierarchy. A low caste was able in a generation or two, to rise to higher position in the hierarchy by adopting vegetarianism and teetotalism, and by Sanskritizing its ritual and pantheon. In short, it took over as far as possible, the customs, rites, and beliefs of the Brahmins and the adoption of the Brahminic way of life by a low caste seems to have been frequent, though theoretically forbidden. This process has been called Sanskritization in this book, in preference to 'Brahminization', as certain Vedic rites are confined to Brahmins and the two other twice-born castes. . . . When this process is viewed on a continental scale and over a period of at least 2,500 years, it is easy to see how Sanskritic ideas and beliefs penetrated the remotest hill tribes in such a manner as not to do violence to their traditional beliefs. Caste enabled Hinduism to proselytize without the aid of a church.[4]

In the words of Milton Singer the formulations of Srinivas were,

> Sanskritization refers essentially to a specific kind of cultural mobility—a mobility that brings groups outside of Hinduism into the fold and raises the cultural status of groups already in it. This cultural mobility takes place within caste system. Non-Hindu groups are Hinduized by becoming castes, and lower castes rise to the cultural status of higher castes as they adopt vegetarianism, teetotal rules and the deities, rites, myths of Sanskritic

> Hinduism as defined in Sanskrit literature and philosophy and as practised by Brahmans. Many groups have thus Hinduized themselves in a generation or two . . . by taking over the customs, rites, and beliefs of the Brahman and other higher castes.[5]

Later Srinivas and others have tried to revise, modify and sharpen the original formulations of Srinivas. In course of that suitability of various other terms like Aryanization, Hinduization and Brahmanization have been discussed as better substitutes of the term Sanskritization but later found unsatisfactory as they only suggest merely one of the multiple aspects of this complex process.[6] Mandelbaum has used the term '*jati* mobility' for this complex process.[7] But as the term Hinduization suggests only the tribal absorption and Hinduization of non-Hindus completely excluding the *jati* mobility from within its semantic range which is just another aspect of the same process, so also the term '*jati* mobility' does not include the concept of tribal absorption and Hinduization which are also parts of the same complex process. It seems not a single term can be used to describe such a complex process. Perhaps compound expressions like 'tribal absorption-cum-*jati* mobility' or 'Hinduization-cum-*jati* mobility' are better suited for the purpose. However, the real focus of this study is not such terminological issue but the workings of this process in a restricted context. Therefore, instead of getting entangled in that sort of problem it will perhaps be worthwhile now to look at this process a little more closely.

Whenever the tribals were absorbed into the Hindu society either they were identified with an earlier existing Hindu *jati* belonging to one of the four *varnas* — brahmana, ksatriya, vaisya and sudra — of the Hindu society or, which was mostly the case, were recognised as a completely new *jati* or separate *jati* in which case their *varna* reference was never explicitly stated and they were generally considered as untouchables. They may be termed here as the fifth *varna*.[8] W.W. Grigson, who studied the process of Hinduization operating among the Kols, made the generalization that the Kols were being regarded by the Hindus as outcaste or scheduled caste.[9] According to him, "The Hinduization of the primitive tribe will eventually lead to their becoming a part of the Hindu social system and then being integrated into its lower strata and becoming regarded by the Hindus as outcaste or scheduled caste."[10] In either case it was often required to define, either precisely or loosely as the case may be, their rank or relative position in the hierarchy of the *jatis* belonging to that *varna*. This identification with an earlier existing Hindu *jati* or recognition as a completely new or separate *jati* and the determination of their rank or relative position in the hierarchy of *jatis* belonging to that *varna* was done through behavioural pattern and/or the transformation of an earlier existing myth, by appropriate modifications, into an 'origin myth' or creation of a completely new 'origin myth' of that *jati*. In the language of Vidyarthi, "such age-contacts . . . have led the tribals to aspire to elevate their status in terms of Hindu caste hierarchy. Three distinct processes have been usually studied and noted (i) the renunciation of certain tribal practices and adoption of others followed by higher castes, (ii) the creation of legends and myths of ancient Hindu tradition and (iii) the exercise of economic and political dominance wherever possible — in seeking recognition to a higher status."[11]

Once absorbed into the Hindu society as a *jati*, the tribal people tended to behave like any other *jati* actively participating in the 'routine politics' (see below for the clarification of this concept) of *jati* mobility, the 'consistent efforts by members of lower *jatis* to raise their ranking', as caste in India is not immutable in practice as some scholars once thought on the basis of ideals and principles. The structural change in the five *varna* system is never allowed whereas positional change (upward/downward movement of a particular *jati* in the five *varna* scale) is allowed though that may not be apparent immediately. This process is termed as *jati* mobility.[12] It does not of course mean that this process of mobility is accepted quietly and easily without any resistance. On the contrary the resistance is rather common and even sometimes vehement whenever/wherever there is a movement for change. But in spite of the resistance the lower *jatis* do succeed in time to raise their rank in the *jati* hierarchy and occasionally (and perhaps as a result of the upward movement of the lower *jati*) the relative position of a higher *jati* in the ladder of the *jati* hierarchy may go down. But, in the words of Mandelbaum, "the social structure remains quite the same even though one group now is accepted as higher than its former superior and its members outrank those of a previously higher set."[13]

According to Mandelbaum the "Routine politics are repetitive, in the sense that whichever side wins, similar conflict at once emerges, and the system goes on as before."[14] Bailey defines it as: "The logistic, factual, and jural rules of this type of conflict are such that when one group wins it is immediately faced with a similar conflict where the same rules apply, and so on down the infinite corridors of structural time, until something happens to change these rules."[15]

It may also be pointed out here that in this constant and consistent effort of upward movement the lower *jatis* are presented with several alternative models, "each with a distinctive complex of vlaues, and that the precise content and the relative rank of these models vary with time and locality." [16] It has been found that the ksatriya model or the 'warrior-ruler model' has been the most popular model for ambitious men of the lower *jatis* in preference to brahmana model.[17]

The following means of cultural adaption may play important roles in the *jati* mobility: the change of the name of the *jati*, social and ritual behaviour, interaction with other *jatis* and origin myth.[18]

A few words regarding the last mentioned means of cultural

adaption may be necessary here as that is quite important for the purpose of the present study. Two different kinds of origin myths are prevalent in the Hindu society: one that gives the account of the creation of the society as a whole and the creation of the four *varna* system as found in *Ṛgveda* and other Hindu scriptures and the other that gives account of the creation of a particular *jati* usually from noble or divine ancestor. The origin myth prevalent in the families or of most of the feudal chiefs of Orissa (as well as other parts of India) may be cited as examples of origin myths of this type. The latter does not usually contradict the former but 'taken in conjunction with it encourages constant competition among jatis'.[19] Besides the tribals may have their own origin myths.

For the purpose of this study it is felt that the question of attributional and interactional criteria for caste-ranking introduced by McKim Marriot is irrelevant.[20] However, regarding that, the position of the present author is quite similar to 'the fourth possibility' of Singer, which is incidentally his own (Singer's) position and that is, 'there is a constant and mutual interpenetration between the two systems, even at the village level'.[21] Therefore, it is not necessary to go into them in any detail as that will not affect the caste-ranking discussed in this study.

In the following pages an attempt will be made to study the highly complex process of tribal absorption-cum-*jati* mobility in medieval Orissa in some detail though in a restricted context.

Notes

1. As for example as early as 1932 L.S.S. O'Malley in no uncertain terms stated, "It is sometimes said that a Hindu is born, not made, that consequently no outsider can be admitted to a Hindu caste and that no one can change his caste. These statements are not quite correct. Hindu castes living in proximity to non-Aryan tribes receive as members new converts to Hinduism. Sir James Lyall wrote in his *Kangra Settlement*

Report : 'On the border line in the Himalayas, between Tibet and India proper, any one can observe caste growing before his eyes; the noble is changing into a Rajput, the priest into a Brahman, the peasant into a Jat, and so on down to the bottom of the scale.' In some areas where there is no sharp dividing line between certain castes, men whose power and means are equal to their ambition may succeed in raising themselves to higher castes." O'Malley, 1974: 32. He had also observed the same phenomena even earlier. In 1908, in Puri District Gazetter, following N.K. Bose he had written, "In other respects, however, the caste system in Orissa appears in some respects to be more loosely organized and more plastic than in Bengal, for it is possible on the one hand for outsiders to be admitted into an already organized caste and on the other, for the members of the same caste to raise themselves to membership of some higher caste. For instance, the Chasās, when they become wealthy, raise themselves to membership of lower classes of Karanas, and assume the respectable title of Mahānti. A common saying is — Bari bari kari Mahānti, chhidi chhidi kari Chasā." O'Malley, 1908: 79.

Earlier N.K. Bose in an article entitled, 'The Hindus of Puri and their Religion' published in 1891 in the *Calcutta Review* had observed, "Hinduism in Orissa holds out to all an ascending scale of ceremonial purity. The backward aboriginal tribes outside the pale of Hinduism, like the Khonds, set up a Hindu god, get a Hindu priest to minister to them, adopt some of the customs of the pure Hindus, and thus become, in time, recognized as low class Hindus. The more energetic, again, of low castes within the pale of Hinduism like the Chasa Od, gradually raise themselves to higher standards of ceremonial purity, and the more wealthy members among them even raise themselves to membership of some higher castes. Not only does Hinduism in Orissa, even at the present time, absorb the less civilized tribes outside its pale, but there is also a process of evolution in active operation among the recongnized Hindu castes themselves." Quoted in O'Malley, 1908: 74.

2. Srinivas, 1965:30. According to Yogendra Singh in the 1952

edition of his book Srinivas had used the term 'Brahmanization' but later preferred to use the term 'Sanskritization' to Brahminization to describe or define this complex process. Singh, Y. 1974: 389.

3. Srinivas, 1965: 24-25.
4. *Ibid.*, 30-31.
5. Singer, 1972: 260-61.
6. ***See*** Kulke, 1976: 1-4 for a brief resume of some of the theoretical discussion on this complex process.
7. Mandelbaum, 1972: 427-30.
8. It may be mentioned here that though following the Vedic tradition the four *varnas* — brahmana, ksatriya, vaisya and sudra — are recognised and untouchables are kept outside the *varna*-system sometimes and especially in south India the untouchables are recognised as 'the fifth' *varna*, 'the *Pancamas*' perhaps for this very reason. ***See*** O'Malley, 1974: 141-42. Srinivas has also recognised 'the division of society into a five-fold hierarchy' and the five *varnas* as has already been shown; ***see*** Srinivas, 1965: 24. According to P.V. Kane this is 'against the *Smrti* tradition' which is proved by the fact that this 'fifth' *varna* has no name. But Kane also admits, "Gradually however, a distinction was made between the Sudras and the castes like Cāṇḍāḷas. Fresh castes were then added to the list of untouchables by custom and usage and the spirit of exclusiveness, though there is no warrant of the sastras for such a procedure." Kane, II, 1, 1941:167-68. Therefore, Mandelbaum's statement, "The converts to Hinduism and untouchables were classed as Shudras" (Mandelbaum, 1972: 449) is not quite correct. Of course, earlier, he also says that the *varna*-scheme "omits from Hindu society the many jatis of so called untouchables." Mandelbaum, 1972: 23.
9. ***See*** Vidyarthi and Rai, 1977: 456.
10. Quoted in Vidyarthi, 1969: 98.
11. Vidyarthi, 1969: 96.
12. ***See*** Srinivas, 1984 and Mandelbaum, 1972: 427-30.

13. Mandelbaum, 1972: 428.
14. Madelbaum, 1972: 428.
15. Quoted in Mandelbaum: 1972: 428.
16. Singer, 1972: 262 and ***see*** also Mandelbaum, 1972: 448-62.
17. Mandelbaum, 1972: 452; ***see*** also Sinha, Surajit, 1962 and Kulke, 1976.
18. Mandelbaum, 1972: 442 ff.
19. ***See*** Mandelbaum, 1972: 429-30.
20. ***See*** Singer, 1972: 262-64 for more information on these criteria and the debates on them.
21. Singer, 1972: 264.

2

Orissa

The Land of the Tribals and the Hindus

ORISSA in eastern India is one of the most ideal places in India to study the tribal absorption into the Hindu society and *jati* mobility as Orissa is the land of the tribals as well as the Hindus and Hindu religion.

It may be mentioned here that in the present discussion Orissa, a state within the Indian Union, represents Orissa, a region, which can be defined culturally, though the boundary of Orissa, the state — which has shrunk considerably from the political boundary of the Orissan empire under Kharavela, in the second century BC or under the Gangas and the Gajapatis between the twelfth and mid-sixteenth centuries — and the boundary of Orissa, the cultural region, which cannot be defined with any precision, may not necessarily correspond to it.

Orissa has a large tribal population. Almost one-fourth of the total population of Orissa is tribal. Some 62 scheduled tribes, most of them speaking a language belonging to either the Dravidian or the Austroasiatic family of languages, live in Orissa. A comparison of the figures of 1961, 1971 and 1981 census makes it amply clear that earlier the percentage of the tribal population to the total population of the Oriya-speaking tract was even higher. According to the 1961 census report the total scheduled tribe population in Orissa was 4,223,757 which comprised 24.07 per cent of the total population of Orissa, the all India figure being 6.86 per cent. In 1971 the respective figures were 5,071,937 and 23.11 per cent and 6.94 per cent. The 1981 figures were 5,915,067 and 22.43 per cent and 7.76 per cent respectively.[1]

Though the tribal population of Orissa is concentrated away from the eastern sea coast and mostly in the northern as well as southern districts one can imagine that once upon a time they were also concentrated in the eastern sea coast. After the advent of the Aryans into Orissa, with their Sanskritic culture, it seems that quite a large number of them got Hinduized and absorbed into the Hindu society though some of them retreated towards the south, north and west, away from the coastal belt where the Aryans first settled. The movement of the Aryans towards the southern, northern and western hinterland was slow and gradual.

Orissa is not only a land of the tribals and tribal religion but also a land of the Hindus and Hindu religion. And one of the most important and holiest, if not the most important and holiest, Hindu shrines, in Lord Jagannatha of Puri, is situated here. Compared to northern India, Hinduism might have come to Orissa much late but it soon made Orissa into a sanctuary of Hinduism, a land of its own. The following observations and remarks by W.W. Hunter, in glowing terms, made in the latter half of the nineteenth century, will amply explain and justify this statement.

"For two thousand years Orissa has been the Holy Land of the Hindus", Hunter declared, "The ancient texts love to dwell on its sanctity. It is 'the land that taketh away sin'."[2]

"Orissa is divided into four great regions of pilgrimage." Hunter further observes, "From the moment the pilgrim passes the Baitarani River, on the high road forty miles north-east of Cuttack, he treads on holy ground. Behind him lies the secular world, with its cares for the things of this life, before him is the promised land, which he has been taught to regard as a place of preparation for heaven. On the southern side of the river rises shrine after shrine to Siva, the All-Destroyer. On its very bank he beholds the house of Yama, the king of the dead; and, as he crosses over, the priest whispers into his ear the last text which is breathed over the dying Hindu at the moment the spirit takes its flight: 'In the dead gloom of Yama's halls is the tepid Baitarani River'. On leaving the stream he enters Jajpur, literally the City of Sacrifice, the headquarters of the region of pilgrimage, sacred to Parvati, the wife of the All-Destroyer. To the south-east is the region of pilgrimage sacred to the sun, now scarcely visited, with its matchless ruins looking down in desolate beauty across the Bay of Bengal. To the south-west is the region of pilgrimage dedicated to Siva, with its city of temples, which once clustered, according to native tradition, to the number of seven thousand, around the sacred lake. Beyond this, nearly due south, is the region of pilgrimage beloved of Vishnu, known to every hamlet throughout India, and to every civilized nation on earth, as the abode of Jagannath, The Lord of the World."

"There is not a Fiscal Division in Orissa," Hunter continues, "without its community of cenobites, scarcely a village without fertile abbey lands, and not a single ancient family which has not devoted its best acres to the gods. Hundreds of monasteries dot the province, and enjoy an aggregate rent roll of £ 50,000 a year. Every town is filled with temples, and every hamlet has its shrine. This lavish devotion extends into the hill country. In going up the Mahanadi, I noticed that each rocky islet, or wooded crag that rose from its banks, was crowned, not, as upon the Rhine, by the castle of a noble, but by a temple to some god. Even foreigners feel that they are treading on hallowed ground, and the villagers still tell how the image-breaking Musalmans retired abashed before the sanctity of Orissa. 'This country is no fit subject for conquest, or for schemes of human ambition, exclaimed the victorious general of Akbar in 1580, it belongs to the gods, and from end to end is one region of pilgrimage.'

This national reverence for holy places has been for ages concentrated on the city of Puri, sacred to Vishnu under his title of Jagannath, the Lord of the World. As the outlying position of Orissa long saved it from conquest, and from that dilapidation of ancient Hindu shrines and rites which marks the Muhammadan line of march through India, so Puri, built upon its extreme south-eastern shore, and protected on the one side by the surf and on the other by swamps and inundations, is the corner of Orissa which has been most left to itself. On these inhospitable sands, Hindu religion and Hindu superstition have stood at bay for eighteen centuries against the world. Here is the national temple whither the people flock to worship from every province of India. Here is the Swargadwara, the Gate of Heaven, whither thousands of pilgrims come to die, lulled to their last sleep by the roar of the eternal ocean. Twenty generations of devout Hindus have gone through life, hunted with a perpetual yearning to visit this shrine. On its fever-stricken sand-hills a nation's adoring love has been lavished. They are Puri, "*the* City of its religious aspirations on earth; they are Purushottama, the dwelling of Vishnu, 'the Best of Men'; they are the symbolical Blue Mountain; they are the mystic naval of the earth."[3]

Besides, at the time of its construction (i.e. the twelfth century) the temple of Jagannatha at Puri was the largest temple in the whole of India, claims G.S. Ghurye.[4] It only emphasizes the importance of Lord Jagannatha in the Hindu world. Further the famous Vedic commentator, Sayana, while commenting on a *sukta* in the *Ṛgveda*, claimed that in the said *sukta* Purushottama-Jagannatha on the sea shore at Puri had been referred to.[5] Sayana or any other Vedic commentator did not ever claim that in Vedic *sukta*s any other Hindu shrine or deity had been referred to as to them it was most unlikely. Therefore, Sayana's discovery of this reference to Purushottama-Jagannatha of Puri in a *sukta* of *Ṛgveda*, however improbable that might be, is quite significant. It only points out the primary importance Lord Jagannatha was given in the whole of the Hindu world during Sayana's time (*circa* AD1300 to1380).

Because of the supreme importance attached to Lord Jagannatha in the whole of the Hindu world and perhaps because the Muslim occupation of Orissa was late and of short duration the Christian missionaries in the nineteenth century considered Puri as the Mecca of the Hindu world and Lord Jagannatha as their greatest enemy in India. No wonder they denounced Jagannatha vehemently, using most offensive and often violent language, in vilest terms under the derisive title, 'Juggernaut'. Claudius Buchana, the first ever Christian missionary to visit Puri in 1806 for the first time, in a speech before Cambridge University declared, "I resolved . . . to visit the chief seat of Hindoo religion for which purpose I made a journey to the great Temple of Juggernaut which is to the Hindoos what Mecca is to Mohammedans, the stronghold fountainhead of their idolatry . . . "[6] Elsewhere he said, "The picture was a terrible one. There on the sand coast of Orissa is a stately Pagoda, grand against the sky, shrine of a mighty Moloch, tended by hundreds of priests and venerated by millions of worhippers."[7] James Peggs, another of them, observed, "a blow at the idolatry here will prove a blow at the root."[8] The *Brief Sketch of the Rise and Progress of Orissa Mission* published in 1858 opens with the sentences, "Orissa is the Palestine of India. What Jerusalem was to the ancient Israelites, that is Pooree to the Hindoos. There the temple of Jaggernath rears its hateful and obscene front."[9] This is quite significant.

In 1880, R.L. Mitra observed, "No Indian divinity has a more unenviable notoriety in English literature than Jaggannatha. Alike in poetry and in prose, in works of imagination as in sober history, he forms a never-dying illustration of all that is cruel, all that is horrible, all that is most revolting to every sense of humanity . . . . It is certain, nevertheless, that human conception has never realized a more innocent and gentle divinity than Jagannatha; and the tenets of his votaries are the very reverse of sanguinary or revolting. In fact never was opprobrium more unjustly cast on an inoffensive object than in this instance, and none merited it less."[10] The only possible explanation or reason behind this most unjustly cast opprobrium is the supreme importance of Jagannatha in whole of the Hindu world.

Because of its large tribal population as well as its supreme importance in the Hindu world and for Hindu religion Orissa should be considered as a suitable and ideal place to study the tribal absorption into the Hindu society and *jati* mobility. But there are even stronger reasons to consider Orissa as the most suitable and ideal location to study the theme.

Firstly some scholars claim that Lord Jagannatha at Puri, the holiest of holy Hindu shrines situated in Orissa, is of tribal origin, however paradoxical that may sound to be, and there are weighty reasons to believe in this theory.[11] Even some Sanskrit *Puranas* admit that the very first worshipper of Jagannatha, in his Nila Madhava form, was a tribal.[12]

Secondly though Orissa, the land of Lord Jagannatha and Hindu religion is considered a home of conservative and orthodox Hinduism, paradoxically enough a certain amount of liberal, tolerant, and even lax attitudes is easily perceptible even within Orissan society. L.S.S.O'Malley, an outsider, observed in 1932, "Orissa is another home of conservatism and orthodoxy, largely because it was long isolated from close contact with the outside world and modernizing influences: the railway was not extended to it till less than half a century ago. The Brahmans punctiliously observe the laws of ceremonial purity but on the other hand the caste system is more fluid than in Madras or Bengal. It is possible not only for outsiders to be admitted into certain low castes but also for men of low caste to rise to higher caste, and intermarriages take place between castes of equal standing and even between some castes of higher and lower rank."[13] He noted, "In Orissa the

Chasas, a clean Sudra caste of agriculturists, admit outsiders, and well-to-do men who are Chasas by birth are sometimes admitted to membership of Karan caste (a twice-born caste corresponding to the Kayasthas of North India) and assume title Mahanti. This custom has given rise to a popular proverb: Rising, rising to Mahanti, falling, falling to Chasa; . . . ."[14] (This may be again due to the late and short duration of Muslim occupation, which is not that relevant here).

Another example of liberal and tolerant attitude incorporated into the conservative and rigid Orissan society is reflected in partaking of the food, even cooked rice, once it is offered to Lord Jagannatha at Puri when it becomes *Mahaprasada*, the holy food. Its sanctity crosses caste or *jati* barriers within the four *varnas* (excluding of course the fifth *varna*, i.e., the untouchables).[15] Therefore, Orissa is considered as the right place to study the tribal absorption and *jati* mobility.

The tribal absorption into the Hindu society in ancient and medieval Orissa took diverse directions and different paths, and it took place in various ways. Hermann Kulke and Anncharlott Eschmann have made some systematic studies on the tribal absorption in Orissa.[16] Kulke has linked it with early state formation in Orissa. Following Burton Stein, who studied the integration of the agrarian system in south India, he has introduced the concept of 'nuclear area' — which was politically and economically independent, self-governing and autonomous and socially and culturally the centre of Hindu civilization — into the discussion on Orissan state formation. According to him unlike in south India, where gradual expansion of the nuclear areas caused a 'sustained displacement of tribally organized pastoral and hunting society of forests and upland areas by caste-organized village based societies', in Orissa the gradual expansion of these nuclear areas — which was necessitated especially by the 'drive towards new arable land' at and beyond the Hindu-tribal frontier — was by gradual 'indoctrination and partial integration' or in other words Hinduization of the tribals.[17] It is not surprising, therefore, that along with the Hinduization of the tribals their tribal deities also got Hinduized. This is an example of Hinduization from below. At the same time another force was also active in the same direction. For both vertical or internal and horizontal or external legitimation the emerging Hindu royalty in the expanding nuclear areas had to extend royal patronage to the tribal deities as well as to construct new stone temples for them. This was frequently the case when the territory in which a deity, having a special connection with that territory, came to be included in the expanding nuclear area over which the Hindu royalty was reigning. According to Kulke "the main reason for this royal patronage was that even a fairly Hinduized court in a tribal or partly Hinduized surroundings, was highly dependent on the support and loyalty of the tribe. Royal patronage of autochthonous deities seem to have been an essential presupposition for the consolidation of political power and its legitimation in the Hindu tribal zone of Orissa."[18]

And as a natural consequence these tribal deities got gradually Hinduized. This was especially true in case of deities who were accepted as tutelary deities, either as state deities (*rastra devata*) of small kingdoms in the nuclear areas or as personal/ family deity (*ista devata*) of the royalty ruling over the nuclear area. In the words of Kulke, "Most of these autochthonous tutelary deities of Orissa underwent a process of Hinduization, the intensity and direction of which usually was directly influenced by the parallel rise of the sub-regional political authority from chieftainship to kingship".[19]

Kulke has further observed that even after these tribal deities were Hinduized, "two important aspects of the cult, however, remained nearly unchanged : the original uniconical symbol of the deity and its priests".[20] What Kulke meant by the latter was that the tribal priests of the Hinduized tribal deities were never, at least not completely, discarded or thrown out and replaced by the Hindu (i.e. the brahmana) priests. This could happen simply because it "served as the ritual bridge between the Hindu rajas and the people who still worshipped the tutelary deity as their own deity".[21] There might have been other reasons as well because many Hinduized or semi-Hinduized tribal deities at the village level, throughout the length and breadth of Orissa, were never made tutelary deities of any Hindu king but the functioning priests attached to these shrines are generally of tribal origin. Eschmann has also cited several such instances where functioning priests of the Hinduized tribal deities are of tribal origin.[22]

Whatever may be the reason or reasons but the fact remains that the original priests of the pre-Hinduized tribal deities were retained and allowed to function as priests even after the Hinduization of the same (i.e. the tribal deities). And their priestly profession quite naturally facilitated their absorption into the Hindu society and even their active participation in the *jati* mobility, their effort to go up in the *jati*-ladder, at a subsequent stage. Therefore the Hinduization of the tribals — a result of several different forces working in that direction — might have been one of the reasons for the Hinduization of tribal deities but that (i.e., the Hinduization of tribal deities) also in turn set in motion a trend which resulted in the Hinduization of a section of tribals, the original priest-worshippers of the subsequently Hinduized tribal deities and their descendants.

Now it will be endeavoured to present this phenomenon, mentioned above, in a broad and generalized theoretical framework — worked out for the purpose — on the basis and in terms of which that (i.e., the phenomenon) can be closely examined and better understood. Moreover the proposed theoretical framework will be quite useful to distinguish this phenomenon from — and also to connect it with — several other similar phenomena.

Among the various channels available to the tribals for Hinduization, for centuries, throughout the length and breadth of Orissa as well as elsewhere in India, one was through their association with a *ksetra*. Here by the term *ksetra* is meant a geographical entity of a few kilometres radius (neither much larger than a city nor much smaller than a village) with some kind of religious sanctity. In other words it is a sacred or holy place containing at least one Hindu religious shrine, which may be a *tirtha*, a deity or some such thing including even a Hinduized tribal deity — the source from which the place derives its religious sanctity.[23] Some of the *ksetras* may have all India recognition like Puri which is known as Sri Purushottama *ksetra* or Sankha *ksetra* while others have only regional or local recognition. In course of time a non *ksetra* may become a *ksetra* as it acquires religious sanctity and *vice-versa*, i.e., a *ksetra* may also lose its religious sanctity — viz. in the event of its desecration — and may become a non-*ksetra*. The former phenomenon may be termed as ksetraization. The formation of a traditional account of *ksetra mahatmya* or *sthala purana* type which invariably grows around any and every Hindu religious shrine or *ksetra* and speaks of its emergence and importance is an important feature of this ksetraization process. Depending on the importance that a *ksetra* may acquire the *ksetra mahatmya* or *sthala purana* may be oral or written in a local or regional language or even written in Sanskrit. In cases of *ksetras* of all India, and in some cases of regional, importance it is even made to form a part of one of the Hindu *Puranas*. Generally the existence of at least one *ksetra* of regional or sub-regional importance in what has been defined as a nuclear area by Burton Stein may be assumed.

The Hinduization of the tribals through their association with a *ksetra* may be termed *ksetra*-centred-Hinduization and may be studied under even a broader heading, *ksetra*-centred-Social Mobility. From among several sub-types of *ksetra*-centred-Hinduization[24] one sub-type stands out from others insofar as it allows the original tribal priests of the pre-Hinduized tribal deity and their descendants to continue to function as priests even after the Hinduization of the deity and to get themselves Hinduized taking advantage of their priestly profession. This particular sub-type of *kṣetra*-centred-Hinduization may be termed as 'pujakaization' (from the Sanskrit word *pujaka* which means worshipper and by extension means priest) in the absence of a better term. Often — though not invariably always — the processes of ksetraization and pujakaization go together, the latter forming a part of the former. This is not at all surprising because whenever a tribal deity gets Hinduized and initiates the process of ksetraization, there is a strong possibility that the original tribal priests of the pre-Hinduized tribal deity will continue to function as priests and will have the opportunity to get themselves Hinduized because of their priestly profession.

The scope of the present work is restricted only to the study, in some detail, of this process of pujakaization, i.e., the absorption of the tribal priests of the Hinduized tribal deities into the Hindu society and their subsequent participation in the *jati* mobility taking advantage of their priestly profession, and the important role played by the origin myth, which has been accepted in this work as a kind of traditional account, in that complex process.

Only this much must be mentioned in that connection here that though the tribal priests of the Hinduized deities were invariably always retained and incorporated into the Hinduized cult as non-brahmana priests at least in some cases — especially in case of the tutelary deities having a special connection with a particular territory (which has been termed 'territoriality' by Kulke)[25] — some kind of Brahmanic take-over was made. The nature and the strength of the Brahmanic take-over was mainly dependent on the political importance of the deity, i.e., the nature and the strength of the 'territoriality' of the deity, and on the nature of the composition of the tribals inhabiting the territory. At the least important village level the Brahmanic take-over was not that necessary. But at the sub-regional or regional level the Brahmanic take-over was very much necessary for the following reasons: (i) in order to commence and continue the more pronounced and more sophisticated Brahmanical form of worship as a part of the Hinduization process (of the tribal deity) especially because the sub-regional or regional nuclear areas were dominated by the brahmanas patronized by the court, (ii) for horizontal or external legitimation against the parallel powers, equivalent rivals and potential challengers, etc.[26]

Further in a few cases the Brahmanic take-over was very much limited to special occasions and to specific periods of the year or time of the day, was confined to only certain rituals and on the whole quite insignificant. Here the non-brahmana priests of tribal origin retained their predominant position in cult affairs and controlled the day-to-day activities of the cult. Sometimes even new temples were constructed near the residence of the royalty for the exclusive use of the brahmana priests where a Brahmanic substitute of the deity was installed to keep the brahmanas in good humour while at the same time leaving the originally tribal but subsequently Hinduized deity in the hands of the non-brahmana priests of tribal origin as in cases of Bhattarika in Baramba and Khilamunda in Ranapur. But in some other cases, especially at subregional or regional level, the Brahmanic take- over was much more pronounced and forceful which pushed the non-brahmana priests into background and to a subsidiary position at least in the day-to-day ritual worship of the deity, restricting their activities, in turn, only to special occasions, to specific periods of the year and time of the day mostly confined to certain rituals, which brought them into the most intimate and personal contact with the deity.

It may be assumed furthermore that whenever the Brahmanic take-over was more pronounced and predominant the necessity for absorption into the Hindu society especially the subsequent upward movement in the *jati* hierarchy was felt more strongly by the non-brahmana priests of tribal origin as they had to compete keenly with the brahmana priests not only for their mere survival but also to raise their social status, economic position and political power.

Much of what have been stated above will be verified in the following pages with an example from medieval Orissan history.

Notes

1. Tripathi, B., 1973 : 299-310; Swain, 1989 : 119, 121-22.
2. Hunter, W.W., Vol. 1, 1872 : 81.
3. *Ibid.*, 82-84.
4. Kulke, H., 1976 : 5 and fn. No. 16.
5. *Ṛgveda*, 10th *Maṇḍala* 155 *Sūkta*, 3rd *Mantra* (10/155/3); ***see*** Padhi, B.M., 1975 : 27-28 and Geib, R., 1975 : 132, fn. No. 448.
6. Quoted in Kulke, H., 1978c : 354.
7. Quoted in Mukherjee, P., 1977 : 205.
8. Quoted in Patra, K.M., 1971 : 249.
9. Quoted in Kulke, H., 1979 : 220 fn. No. 24.
10. Mitra, R. L., 1963 : 167.
11. ***See*** Padhi, B.M. 1975; Geib, R., 1975 and Eschmann, A., 1978b : 99.
12. ***See*** *Purusottama Mahatmya* of *Skanda Purana* and *Niladri Mahodaya*.
13. O'Malley, L. S. S., 1974 : 22-23.
14. *Ibid.*, 32-33; ***see*** also above chapter 1, note no. 1 in this connection.
15. Hunter making really a tall claim says, "Its sanctity over leaps all barriers, not only caste, but of race and hostile faith; and I have seen Puri priest put to the test of receiving the food from a Christian's hand." Hunter, W.W., Vol. 1, 1872 : 86.
16. ***See*** Eschmann, A., 1978a and 1978b; Kulke, H., 1978a and 1978b.
17. Kulke, H., 1978a : 126-29, 136; 1979 : 224-27, 14-26.
18. ***See*** Kulke, H., 1978a : 129; 1979 : 25-26, 227 for detailed discussion on this topic.

19. Kulke, H., 1978a : 130; ***See*** also Kulke, H., 1979 : 227.
20. Kulke, H., 1978a : 130-31; ***see*** also Kulke, H., 1979 : 227.
21. Kulke, H., 1978a : 131.
22. ***See*** Eschmann, A., 1978a : 86, 93-97; 1978b : 105.
23. Regarding the term *ksetra* I do not agree with Sontheimer when he says, "By ksetra I mean inhabited, well-settled space with regular plough agriculture, the village in such space e.g. the agrahara villages in coastal Karnataka or sasana villages in Orissa, and the holy centres connected with them." (Sontheimer, 1987 : 127) or, "... the nuclear areas of agriculture" (Sontheimer, 1987 : 138) following Burton Stein and contrasts the same (i.e. the term *ksetra*) with the term *vana*. (**See** Sontheimer, 1987 : 117-64). It will be much more appropriate to contrast the Sanskrit term *janàpada* with the term *vana* and substitute the same for the term *ksetra* in the sense Sontheimer wants to use it. Similarly, to me, the term *ksetra* must have some kind of religious importance or significance, however less or meagre that may be, about which Sontheimer is not very particular. Kulke has used the term *tirtha* instead of *ksetra* to mean sacred place. **See** Kulke, 1978a : 132-33. But *tirtha* is only a specific type of sacred place which derives its religious sanctity from a body of holy water especially a stream or river. (For this reason the sea is sometimes called *tirtha-raja*, i.e., the king among the *tirthas*.) But all the sacred places do not necessarily derive their religious sanctity from a body of holy water. That means all the *tirthas* may be *ksetras* but reverse is not true, i.e., all the *ksetras* may not necessarily be *tirthas*. Therefore the term *ksetra* is considered more appropriate than the term *tirtha*. Dhal has used the term *ksetra* precisely in the sense it is used in this work and has supplied some information on some of the important *ksetras* of Orissa. **See** Dhal, U.N., 1992 : 121-24. The use of the term *ksetra mahatmya* also supports my contention.
24. **See** Kanaka Durga and Sudhakar Reddy for an example of a different type of *ksetra*-centred-Hinduization.
25. Kulke, H., 1979 : 225-26, 8-9.
26. **See** Kulke, H., 1978a : 136-37 and 1979 : 227 for explanation of the term 'horizontal legitimation'.

3

Traditional Account

A Source of History

BESIDES the study of the absorption of the tribal priests into the Hindu society and their subsequent participation in the *jati* mobility in the Orissan context and the role of the origin myth — treated here as just a kind of traditional account — in that process, which are its primary concerns, this work seeks to initiate two novel trends in the field of Orissan historiography:

(i) to lay more emphasis on the importance of traditional account as a source material in the reconstruction of history especially the religion-centered history of the medieval period; and

(ii) to introduce a radically new and different method of analysing the same (i.e., traditional account) as a historical source material.

This concern for the traditional account as a source material emanates firstly from one of the primary concerns of this work, i.e., from the study of the role of the origin myth, which is treated here as a kind of traditional account, in the absorption of the tribals into the Hindu society as well as their subsequent participation in the *jati* mobility, and secondly — which though again a corollary of the former has also independent validity — from the fact that different versions of a particular traditional account has been accepted as a major source material for the present study. Therefore, a brief general discussion and theoretical orientation on the importance of the traditional account as a historical source material, as well as the new method of analysing it especially in the Orissan context will not be considered out of place here.

Traditional account, be it oral or written, legendary/semi-legendary or mythical/semi-mythical, is quite important as source material especially to study and understand the structure of medieval society and workings of medieval mind. As the traditional account reflects the interaction of the forces and counter-forces in the collective sub-conscious mind of the society and registers the inner movements and the subtle stirrings in it, it can certainly help to develop an insight grasping the magnitude of even the minutest movement. Therefore, the traditional account should be considered even better than other types of source materials like official documents, inscriptions, etc., which are at best likely to present only a one-sided picture.[1]

Although this view may not be completely new there has been a tendency lately to minimize the importance of the traditional account as one of the source materials and to ignore it at the slightest pretext in the context of Orissan historiography. If at all used, it is used as corroborative evidence and at times with obvious reluctance to fill in small gaps. Scholars tend to reject the account if it is not supported by any other evidence especially inscriptional evidence. It goes without saying that the supernatural elements in it are considered absurd and confusing, and are rejected with contempt. This trend was set by M.M. Chakravarti[2] and J.F. Fleet[3] at the end of the last century, while discussing the historicity of *Madala Panji*,[4] the Chronicle of the Jagannatha temple, Puri, as a reaction to an earlier trend which tended to accept traditional account *in toto* as a piece of history and to believe almost everything in it as truth.

Of course, the traditional account can neither be accepted nor rejected in its entirety as a source material of history which has been the case in Orissan historiography thus far. It must be subjected to the rigours of scientific analysis especially adopting the concepts and methodology of ethnology and sociology as tools and the result must then be compared with the information derived from the source materials other than the traditional account so that the substratum of truth in the traditional account, running like an undercurrent hidden from the eye, can be discovered. One of the very first steps in that direction is to ask what has/have been its, and its different versions', if they exist, function/functions[5] instead of asking if there had been a historical basis of the tradition. In other words one must ask what purpose/purposes the traditional account ever served/now serves? This question must be asked even if the traditional account had a historical basis and more so if it had not any and it is completely fabricated as is often alleged. The same question must also be asked regarding the different versions of the same tradition when more than one version exists. In other words one must try to find out for what reason(s) the original tradition emerged in the first place and then — if at all — got altered and modified which constantly happens in case of a traditional account; one must try to find out the reason(s) behind the emergence of a traditional account and alterations and modifications through which it constantly passes; one must try to find out for what reason(s) a tradition and then different versions of it came into being. Incidentally this can be best done by comparing and contrasting several versions of a particular tradition and then trying to reconstruct the original or the proto-tradition applying the principles of comparative reconstruction, which is being used in historical linguistics to reconstruct the proto-language quite successfully since the middle of the last century, to the possible extent. And particularly if a rough chronology of the different versions of a traditional account is known that can provide interesting suggestions in discovering the reason(s) behind each of the different versions. The purpose behind a traditional account and its different versions, when such versions exist, can be discovered by asking which individual or which group benefited — and when more than one individual or group benefits which one benefited the most — from it. As the individual always belongs to a group and represents its interests it is the group — be it economic, political, religious, social or any other type of group — that really matters in the final or ultimate analysis. The related questions that may be asked in order to discover this group interest is to ask with which group the tradition originated? Which group maintained, preserved and transmitted the same? Which group was responsible for its modification/alteration or emergence of another version of the same tradition? When did it originate or emerge or came into being or was born for the first time? Why did it emerge/originate only then?

After the traditional accounts are subjected to such questions one can hope to draw a more complete and satisfactory picture of the religion centred medieval society. This generalization is more applicable in case of mythical/semi-mythical traditions as these have a very special place in every ancient and medieval religion and as such are likely to throw much light on some dark corners which otherwise may remain enveloped in darkness.

This is even more true in case of medieval Orissa as the source material at our disposal to study that period of Orissan history is both scanty and fragmentary. But in Orissan historiography such method to analyse the traditional account has almost never been attempted. Further the traditional account as source material virtually remains ignored and neglected.[6]

After this general discussion on the importance of the traditional account as a historical source material and the new method of analysing the same, now a few hypothetical observations on the nature of the origin myth type of traditional account will make the discussion more complete and meaningful and at the same time pave the way for the ongoing discussion on the primary concern of this work.

It has already been mentioned that the origin myth plays an important role in the tribal absorption as well as in the *jati* mobility. It appears that in the tribal absorption and the *jati* mobility either a completely new origin myth is created or an earlier existing traditional account—irrespective of its legendary or mythical character (and which may even have been another origin myth, i.e., telling the origin of something else)—is suitably modified to cater to the need. In case of the Pujakaization type of *ksetra*-centred-Hinduization, i.e., Hinduization of the tribal priests resulting out of the Hinduization of the tribal deity, it is quite natural that the Hinduized tribal deity is made to play a significant role in the origin myth which after all deals with the origin of a section of priests—even if of tribal origin—of the same deity. In the origin myth the Hinduized tribal deity either serves as a linkage between the priests of the tribal origin on one hand and the Hindu society on the other facilitating a smooth transition in the absorption of the former in the latter or provides direct or indirect support to the newly Hinduized priests of tribal origin softening the vehemence of opposition to them in their upward mobility in the *jati*-ladder.

As the Hinduized tribal deity is made to play a significant role in the origin myth of a section of priests of the same deity albeit of tribal origin it is small wonder that the origin myth quite naturally gets incorporated and interwoven into a larger traditional account, either pre-existent or due to emerge at a future point of time, of *sthala purana* or *ksetra mahatmya* type which centres round that particular deity. In the process the traditional account deriving out of the *sthala purana* or *ksetra mahatmya* gets modified and restructured.

It should perhaps be mentioned here that the *sthala purana* or *ksetra mahatmya* type of traditional account which invariably grows around any and every Hindu religious shrine including the Hinduized tribal deity may also be treated as another kind of origin myth as it primarily deals with the emergence and importance of the Hindu shrine. Sometimes it is even made to form part of the Hindu *Purana* literature written either in Sanskrit representing the 'great tradition' or in a regional or local language representing the 'little tradition' to use Redfield's rather famous though unsatisfactory terminology.[7]

The nature and character of the origin myth and especially its significant role or function in the tribal absorption and *jati* mobility in the specific area of *ksetra*-centred-Hinduization process have so far neither been examined in any detail nor assumed and understood far less verified, at least not in the context of Orissan historiography. An attempt at studying this aspect will be made in the following pages.

Notes

1. Jan Vansina observes, "There is no great difficulty in accepting the proposition that history is always an interpretation. . . . Thus every historian is obliged to interpret the sources he is dealing with. He does not and cannot have an ultimate knowledge of history and there is usually more than one interpretation possible of the facts at his disposal . . . it follows that there is no such thing called 'absolute historical truth' and no one can formulate an 'unchanging law of history' on the basis of the our knowledge of the past. The truth always remains beyond our grasp, and we can only arrive at some approximation to it. We can refine our interpretations, accumulate so many probabilities that they almost amount to certainty, and yet still not arrive at 'the truth'. . . . What the historian can do is to arrive at some approximation to the ultimate historical truth. He does this by using calculations of probability, by interpreting the facts and by evaluating them in an attempt to recreate for himself the circumstances which existed at certain given moments of the past. And here the historian using oral traditions finds himself on exactly the same level as historians using any other kind of historical source material. No doubt he will arrive at a lower degree of probability than would otherwise be attained, but that does

not rule out the fact that what he is doing is valid, and that is history." (Vansina, Jan, 1965:183-86). But the position of the present author is a little different from Vansina's. The present author does not believe that the traditional account as a source material of history will lead to a lower degree of probability. On the contrary he believes that it will fill in certain gaps and will throw light on certain areas which will otherwise remain unfilled and dark. The present author will like to compare a traditional account with any archaeological material. Much corroded and consequently much modified archaeological remains, even if broken to pieces, can still reveal useful and valuable information and throw light on the past; similarly much altered, much modified and even restructured traditional account or even a single motif of it can supply valuable and useful information.

2. For Chakravarti's view, ***see*** Acharya, P., 1969a: 553-56. In a paper read in a meeting of the Asiatic Society of Bengal in 1891, which was published in the journal of the Society in 1895, Chakravarti observed, "The Madala Panji or the chronicle of the Jagannath Temple is almost the only source; but unless corroborated, its statements cannot be fully relied upon." Chakravarti, 1895: 128. In another paper read in a meeting of the Society in 1892, and published in the journal of the Society in 1893, he further observed, "In spite of the researches of Stirling, Princep, Hunter and Rajendralal Mitra, the history of Orissa was very obscure. The Madala Panji was still its main basis and the Madala Panji was very unsafe and confusing guide, being itself based on unsatisfactory, imperfectly recorded, and often contradictory traditions. The work should be deposed from the high pedestal which it now occupies and placed in its proper rank, as a corroborative document only." (Quoted in Acharya, P., 1969a : 554). In another article read before the Society in 1897 and published in 1898 Chakravarti observed, "The historical value of Madala Panji has been very much over-rated. The original information were often not correctly entered. Then again the chronicle being on the palm-leaves, it had to be recopied three or four times in a century, and in recopying many mistakes crept in, particularly in

figures. Lastly the Seba (worship) was closed several times on account of the Mohomadan raids, and many volumes must have been lost at the time. Hence the text is found full of mistakes and cannot be relied upon, unless corroborated by other evidence . . .

N.B.: Since writing this article, a kind letter of Dr. Fleet has drawn my attention to his remarks on the *Madala Panji* in the *Epigraphia Indica.* Dr. Fleet has analysed the earliest list of kings carefully and come to the conclusion that the annal is 'absolutely worthless for any purposes of ancient history' (p. 335). I came nearly to the same conclusion when I was studying the original manuscript of Madala Panji. In an article read before this Society an abstract of which was published in the Proceedings for July 1892, I noticed the general unreliability of the historical portion of the Madala Panji, and remarked that at best it can be used only as a corroborative document. Dr. Fleet's analysis confirms me in that view." Chakravarti, 1898b : 376-77.

(***See*** also Acharya, P., 1969a : 555). Chakravarti continued in the same vein to demolish the authenticity of *Madala Panji* and in another paper written in 1903 he remarked, ". . . it proved the un-authenticity of the chronology of the Ganga kings as recorded in Madala Panji."(quoted in Acharya, P. 1969a : 556).

3. Fleet in a paper published in 1894/95, made the following observations on *Madala Panji*, ". . . these annals are in reality absolutely worthless for any purposes of ancient history" (Fleet, J.F., 1894/95 : 335) and ". . . it is evident that everything relating to ancient times, which has been written on the unsupported authority of these annals, has to be expunged bodily from the pages of history." (*Ibid.*, 338).

4. For more information of *Madala Panji* ***see*** Chand, R.P., 1927; Panigrahi, K.C., 1981: 122-29; and Kulke, H., 1987a and 1987b.

5. It should be made clear at this place that the term 'function' used here should not be confused with the term 'function' used by the functionalist anthropologists. As far as traditional

accounts are concerned the position of the functionalist anthropologists who reject any oral tradition, even when it forms the basis of a written tradition, as historical data (***see*** Vansina, J., 1965:12-14) is different from the position held by the present author.

6. The only exceptions to this state of affairs are Pandit Nilakanth Das and K.C. Panigrahi who in recent times have made use of traditional accounts to reconstruct the history of Orissa. But only Pandit Nilakantha Das whose writings, mostly in Oriya, are ignored by the professional historians, has developed some insight into the nature and purpose of the traditional accounts while using the same to reconstruct the literary and cultural history of Orissa (***see*** Das, Pandit Nilakanth, 1967). Panigrahi, in spite of his brilliance in analysing the traditional accounts, has followed the conventional method of discovering only the historical basis of the traditional accounts (***see*** Panigrahi, K.C., 1963). Pyarimohan Acharya, a nineteenth-century historian, while reconstructing the history of the fifteenth century Orissa concerning the succession of Purusottam Dev to the throne, has hinted at the possible function which a particular traditional account might have served (***see*** Acharya, Pyarimohan, 1925: 80). The present author in several of his papers written both in Oriya and English and a monograph written in Oriya has made use of the new method to analyse the traditional accounts of Orissa (***see*** Bibliography).

7. For more information on Redfield's terminologies and concepts of great tradition and little tradition, ***see*** Singer, 1972: 3-10.

4

The Nila Madhava-Jagannatha

Tradition at a Glance

THE different versions of the traditional account of *sthala purana* or *ksetra mahatmya* type, referred to here as the Nila Madhava-Jagannatha tradition and accepted as the major source material for this study, are to be found in two interrelated groups of texts: (i) Sanskrit texts like the *Brahma Purana*, the *Purusottama Mahatmya* of the *Skanda Purana*, *Niladrimahodaya*, etc. which, to use Redfield's terminology, are parts of the 'great tradition' and may be called as Brahmanic versions and (ii) Oriya texts like the *Mahabharata* by Sarala Das and the *Deula Tola* texts by Sisu Krsna Das, etc. which, again in Redfield's terminology, are parts of the 'little tradition' and may be called here as non-Brahmanic or folk versions.[1] The traditional account purports to tell how Lord Jagannatha came to be worshipped at Puri.

It ought to be made clear at the very outset, in this connection, that the basic purpose behind this study is not to analyse the Nila Madhava-Jagannatha tradition thoroughly or in its entirety, in all its aspects. This tradition has already been analysed very thoroughly to discover the origin and history of the cult of Jagannatha by Ruprecht Geib in his work, *Indradyumna-Legende: Ein Beitrag zur Geschichte des Jagannatha-kultes.*[2] The purpose of this work is rather limited only to the study of tribal absorption-cum-*jati* mobility in the medieval Orissa in a restricted context as this aspect has not been dealt with by Geib. Although he has been able to touch some of the subtle points and discover some of the significant facts which are quite relevant, he has not been able to grasp their real implications in his otherwise excellent work as his purpose was different. At best he has been able to interpret some of them in a way which is quite different from the interpretations to be made in this study. This is not at all surprising considering Geib's Indological and Sanskritic background.

Therefore only those folk or Oriya versions of this tradition which are considered to be more relevant to study tribal absorption and *jati* mobility will be analysed in some detail and Brahmanic or Sanskrit versions of the tradition will only be referred to whenever necessary merely for the sake of comparison with the Oriya versions. And, as has already been mentioned, these non-Brahmanic or folk versions of this tradition are to be found in the following two Oriya texts:

(i) *Mahabharata* by Sarala Das (hereafter *Sarala Mahabharata*)

(ii) *Deula Tola* by (Sisu) Krsna Das.

The former, generally accepted as a fifteenth-century work, is not at all a mere translation of the famous Sanskrit *Mahabharata*. Retaining the main story of the Sanskrit text more or less intact Sarala Das, the Oriya poet, has really written a *Mahabharata* on his own in Oriya. In the process he has made many additions, deletions, alterations and modifications in the story of *Mahabharata* as recorded in the original Sanskrit text. Because of that, scholars have even claimed that Sarala Das has incorporated his contemporary as well as the past political and military events consciously and deliberately in his *Mahabharata* in the mythological guise transforming the same into the different episodes of *Mahabharata*.[3] Even if this claim is considered too tall or exaggerated or even completely dismissed as unfounded it cannot be denied that at least the interaction of the contemporary social, religious, political and economic forces and counter-forces found reflection in the *Sarala Mahabharata* perhaps without the conscious effort or even the knowledge of its author which is quite natural. Therefore, *Sarala Mahabharata* may be considered as an ideal source material to verify the hypothetical statements concerning the tribal absorption into the Hindu society made earlier. The above-mentioned Nila Madhava-Jagannatha tradition occurs in two different sections (*parbas*) of *Sarala Mahabharata*, the *Bana parba* and the *Musali parba*, which have been accepted as major source materials for the present study. The *Bana parba* version of the tradition is rather brief but in the *Musali parba* the tradition has been treated rather elaborately. Besides this there are also factual differences between both the versions of the same tradition occurring in the same text.[4]

Deula Tola, which literally means, 'the construction of the temple' is an expression generally applied to a group of texts, rather than a single text, having many of the characteristics of *Ksetra Mahatmya* but originating in the little tradition. This group consists of some seven to eight known texts, but there may be some more texts the existence of which is not yet known and yet to be discovered. Most of these texts have the common title (*Purusottama*) *Deula Tola* though a few are titled as *Daru Brahma* (*Purana*/*Gīta*). There are close similarities, in spite of the differences in details, among the texts belonging to this group. This is not at all surprising as the aim of these texts was the same, i.e., to cater to the needs of the pilgrims as well as the general public. That being so the subject-matter and the story structure, the narration and even sometimes the language and style more or less follow the same line. Sometimes even many of the lines are common. Therefore, it appears that different texts belonging to this group are just different versions of a single text prepared by persons representing interests of various groups. This is an example of how different versions — even if the difference is not too apparent and is outwardly slight — of the same text are prepared with different purposes which they serve, sometimes admirably. Most probably these texts have been authored by persons who were not contemporary to one another. Besides this, nothing is known about their precise dates, not even their relative chronology. It is sometimes assumed that the earliest of this group of texts — which may be called the proto-text — has been authored by one Nilambar Das. If this Nilambar Das can be identified with the Nilambar Das who translated the *Kriyayogasara* section of Sanskrit *Padma Purana* into Oriya under the title *Haribhaktiratnamala* and wrote some other works, then, most probably, he belonged to the later seventeenth century.[5] But the *Deula Tola* text supposedly written by Nilambar Das is neither available in print nor in manuscript form. Therefore, the existence of a *Deula Tola* text by Nilambar Das is extremely doubtful. If at all it ever existed it is now lost.[6] Among the other texts of this group, supposedly posterior to the yet undiscovered text by Nilambar Das, two texts, one bearing the title, *Daru Brahma* (*Gita*) and the other named *Deula Tola*, have been written by one (Sisu) Dama Das.[7] Most probably this Dama Das also belonged to the late seventeenth century.[8] Besides texts written by Magunia, Dinabandhu and (Sisu) Krsna Das belong to this group.[9] It is assumed that all these texts have been written between mid-seventeenth century and late eighteenth or even mid-nineteenth centuries, i.e., two to three hundrd years after *Sarala Mahabharata*.

For the purpose of this study *Deula Tola* by (Sisu) Krsna Das has been selected, from among the texts belonging to this group, as a source material. This is because this text especially supplies the information that is required for the verification of the hypothetical statements made earlier. Secondly this text stands out from among the other similar *Deula Tola* and *Daru Brahma* texts because of its extreme popularity. This is the only text of this group which has been printed in the Oriya script, published several times by several publishers in recent times and is available in the market in printed form. Therefore it is well that this particular text has been selected as a source material to represent *Deula Tola* group of texts. But it must be mentioned here that even this particular text, belonging to a group of similar texts, has different versions or readings.[10]

Though there are major as well as minor differences existing among the various versions and sub-versions of this tradition, i.e., between the Sanskritic or Brahmanic version on the one hand and the non-Brahmanic or folk version on the other and then among the sub-versions belonging to each of the versions, which has been mentioned above, the story structure of the traditional account more or less runs as follows:

A chief of an aboriginal tribe, the Savaras (the corresponding Oriya term is Sabara) worshipped a deity named Nila Madhava, a form of god Visnu, secretely in a hilly area named Nilagiri geographically supposed to be located in or near present-day Puri. The name of this Savara chief is Visva Vasu (the corresponding Oriya form is Bisva Basu) according to most of the versions but Jara *alias* Basu according to *Sarala Mahabharata*. A Hindu king of north India sent a brahmana explorer in search of the deity whom he wanted to worship. According to most of the versions the brahmana explorer is named Vidyapati (the corresponding Oriya form is Bidyapati) but according to *Sarala Mahabharata* his name was Basu (the corresponding Sanskrit form is Vasu). The name of the Hindu king is Indrayumna according to most of the versions but according to the *Bana parba* version of *Sarala Mahabharata* his name is Gala or Galaba. The Hindu king having been informed of the secret existence of Nila Madhava by the brahmana explorer Vidyapati came with an army to worship the deity. But the deity vanished miraculously and the Savara chief was deprived of worshipping the deity. Later the deity re-appeared but in the form of a holy log (*daru*) out of which the king got the images of Jagannatha, Balabhadra and Subhadra (and also Sudarsana) carved. The king then consecrated the images according to the Brahmanic scripture, worshipped them and thus founded the cult of Jagannatha at Puri.[11]

This story structure has some resemblance with the family histories of many of the feudal chiefs (the feudatory *rajas*) of Orissa which has not escaped Hunter's notice.[12] According to these family histories—which have more or less a common story structure — a ksatriya prince/chieftain/scion of a royal family of north India comes to Orissa either as a fugitive or as an adventurer or on a pilgrimage to Puri, the abode of Lord Jagannatha, then ceremonially kills a (tyrannous) tribal chief of a locality and finally establishes/lays foundation of a kingdom making the killed or martyred tribal chief the *ista devata* or the presiding deity of the newly established/founded kingdom of that locality becoming its first king.[13]

Notes

1. For more information regarding the different versions of the Nila Madhava-Jagannatha tradition, ***see*** Padhi, 1975: 1-3; Mishra, 1971 and Geib, 1975. For more information on Redfield's concepts of the Great and Little Traditions, ***see*** Singer, 1972: 3-10.
2. Geib, 1975.
3. Though scholars like Mrutyunjaya Rath, Gopinath Nanda-Sharma and Pandit Nilakanth Das had made similar observations earlier it is K.C. Panigrahi who elaborated and made serious efforts to establish this point. For claims by Rath, Nanda-Sharma and Das, ***see*** Dash, G.N. 1988: 2-3. For Panigrahi's elaborations and arguments ***see*** Panigrahi, 1958-60; 1975 and 1976. Dash has also challenged some of Panigrahi's contentions. ***See*** Dash, G.N., 1988.
4. ***See*** Geib, 1975: 137-75 for more information.
5. Mahapatra, K.N., 1969: 157-58. Surya Narayana Das has not been able to fix his time though he has dealt with him and his works at the very end of the Maratha period, i.e., between 1751 and 1803 in his history of Oriya literature. ***See*** Das, S.N. 1966:

721-22. B.M. Padhi claims that Nilambar Das belonged to the fifteenth century. ***See*** Padhi, 1975: 160. But he has not supported his claim with any evidence.

6. B.M. Padhi claims, of course, that he had seen a palm-leaf manuscript of *Deula Tola* text supposedly written by Nilambar Das of the fifteenth century. ***See*** Padhi, 1975: 160. But he has not furnished any other information about this manuscript and does not say where it was available. His claim is extremely doubtful. [In a private discussion he once mentioned that he has seen the printed text of *Deula Tola* by Nilambar Das in the (presently Government) College Library at Parlakhimedi. But this printed text is not traceable at the moment].

7. W.W. Hunter had noticed the "Daru Brahma" and has reproduced the Daru Brahma version of the tradition in his work claiming, it "has wide circulation in Oriya vernacular" (Hunter, Vol. I, 1872: 89). It seems at another place of his work he has mentioned this particular text under the slightly expanded title of *Daru Brahman Gita* and ascribes the authorship of it to one Sisu Dama Das. (**See** Sahu, N.K., ed., 1956a: 220). He has also mentioned another text named *Deula Tola* with the remark that its authorship is doubtful. (**See** Sahu, N.K., ed., 1956a: 221). An Oriya text under the title, *Śrīkṣetra Mahatmya ba Deula Tola* has been printed several times in the Bengali script at the Nihar Press, Kanthi, in the District of Midnapore, West Bengal. More than one such edition is available at the National Library, Calcutta. At the end of the second canto or chapter (*adhyaya*) of the Kanthi edition of the work the authorship of the work has been ascribed to one Damu Das. An Oriya text named *Daru Brahma* the authorship of which has been ascribed to Dama Das has been appended to Orissa Research Project manuscript of *Harivamsa* by Narayana Das. This text, in some respects, differs from the Kanthi edition text.

8. Mahapatra, K.N., 1969: 165.

9. Surya Narayan Das claims that Balaram Das, the early sixteenth century author of the famous *Jagamohana Ramayana* or *Dandi Ramayana*, has also authored a *Deula Tola* text. **See**

Das, S.M., 1967: 74 fn. But he has not supplied any other information on this text. K.C. Sahu, retired Professor of Oriya, Utkal University, has in his private collection several palm-leaf manuscripts of the *Deula Tola* text by Magunia Das. He has kindly provided me with a paper copy of one of such manuscripts. It differs from the other *Deula Tola* texts in another respect, i.e., it is written in nine-syllabic metre whereas the other texts are written in fourteen-syllabic metre. K.N. Mahapatra in his unpublished, *Devotional Reference to Jagannath in Old Oriya Literature* notices a *Deula Tola* text by one Dinabandhu. Mahapatra, K.N., 1973: 96. *Deula Tola* by Sisu Krsna Das is available in the printed form.

10. I have three different versions of this text published by three different publishers: Dasarathi Pustakalaya, Cuttack, Prabhati Pustakalaya, Cuttack and Orissa Kohinoor Press, Cuttack. Each version is slightly different from the other two. Two more Cuttack publishers, Dharma Grantha Store and Orissa Jagannath Company, have also published the *Deula Tola* text by (Sisu) Krsna Das. ***See*** Geib, 1975: 159, fn. 521.

11. For more information ***see*** Padhi, 1975; Geib, 1975; and Mishra, 1971.

12. Hunter, W.W., Vol. 1, 1872: 94.

13. Kulke, H., 1976.

5

The Tribal Priests of a Hindu Shrine

ON the basis of the Nila Madhava-Jagannatha tradition and other evidences a number of scholars have tried to trace and establish the tribal origin of the cult of Jagannatha which has been accepted in this study. According to these scholars the deity which was being worshipped, as per the tradition, by the tribal chief was really not an Aryan deity, though in different versions of the tradition the deity is called Nila Madhava. It was in fact a tribal deity and this tribal deity, in course of time, was Hinduized and transformed to become the Lord Jagannatha of today. The name Nila Madhava was given to its earlier form worshipped by the tribal chief only as a matter of strategy in order to pave the path of its smooth transition from a tribal deity to a Hindu deity, in order to facilitate the process of Hinduization and transformation and perhaps also with a view to neutralize and effectively counter any future opposition to its legitimation as a Hindu deity.[1]

It is irrelevant for the purpose of this study to determine whether the process of Hinduization started from below, i.e., by the tribals worshipping their tribal deity, or from above, i.e., by the brahmanas and/or the kings or chieftains. It may be that the efforts were made simultaneously from both the sides. Geib has shown that though a section of orthodox brahmanas had opposed the recognition and acceptance of this tribal deity, another section of brahmanas had indeed come forward to recognise and accept it and even to contribute positively to its legitimation and Hinduization.[2]

This transformation of a tribal deity into a Hinduized deity of all India Brahmanic recognition released certain forces, initiated certain processes and unleashed certain actions and reactions one of which is the tribal absorption into the Hindu society.

The Hinduization of this tribal deity provided an opportunity to the tribal worshippers or priests (of this Hinduized deity) to get themselves absorbed into the Hindu society. With the Hinduization of the deity the Brahmanic rites were gradually introduced and consequently brahmana priests were also engaged to carry on the worship as per the prescription of the Hindu scriptures. But—it may be further assumed that—the original tribal worshippers or priests just could not be completely ignored or thrown out and their descendants' rights and privileges to worship this Hinduized tribal deity could not be outrightly rejected and had to be recognized though that might have been restricted in course of time. It is probable that the original tribal priests and their descendants were accorded priestly or semi-priestly recognition or at least very high status in the newly Hinduized cult side by side with newly engaged brahmana priests. Kulke citing analogous cases has shown why or how the worshippers/priests of other tribal deities of Orissa were accepted as priests in the Hinduized cults.[3]

It should be mentioned here that there are 118 categories of the temple servants (*sevaka*) performing different religious and ritual duties/services in the temple of the Lord Jagannatha at Puri according to the Record-of-Rights besides the services performed by different monasteries (*matha*) and by certain individuals.[4] Out of these 118 categories of the temple servants only a few categories can be accorded the priestly or semi-priestly recognition and status. It seems 'the Daitas' and 'the

Sudha Suaras' (sometimes written as Suddha/Sudu/Suda Suara and which includes the category Anasara Sudha/Suddha/Sudu/Suda Suaras), the two important categories from among the 118 categories of temple servants who have been accorded either priestly or semi-priestly recognition and status (or at least very high status) in the hierarchy of the temple servants are almost certainly of tribal origin, the descendants of the original tribal worshippers or priests.

The functions or the ritual duties and services of the Daitas as the temple servants are many which cannot be described here in any detail. Apart from their services on a few other occasions their chief or real functions or ritual services commence from the eve of *Snana Yatra*, i.e., the bathing-ceremony which falls on the full-moon day of the lunar month of Jyestha in the Hindu calendar and continue till the end of the car festival. After the bathing ceremony is over the three deities of the temple of Jagannatha at Puri are taken from the bathing platform to the Anasara enclosure which only the Daitas and Patis (or Pati Mahapatras) — another section or category of the temple servants, the supposedly Brahmanic counterpart of the tribal or non-Brahmanic Daitas — can enter. No other person or category of the temple servants, not even the regular brahmana priests such as the *Pujapandas*, is allowed inside the Anasara enclosure. The Daitas along with the Patis perform or at least participate in the ritual worship of the deities inside the Anasara enclosure till the commencement of the car-festival, a period of roughly two weeks. During the car-festival the Daitas perform most of the ritual services. Among these some important and special services are *pahandi*, i.e., taking the deities in a procession to their cars and back in a swinging manner, etc. Further, during the *Navakalevara* or the periodic renewal of the wooden images (of the deities) the Daitas along with the Patis perform most of the ritual services and especially those which are supposed to be secret. In some of these services the Patis take precedence over the Daitas whereas in some other the Daitas take precedence over the Patis.[5]

As to the priestly or semi-priestly status of the Daitas in the hierarchy of the temple servants it should be pointed out here that they are the counterpart of the Patis or Pati Mahapatras, who are indisputedly priests and as per the age-old custom the Daitas serve the left side of each of the images of Lord Jagannatha, Balabhadra, Subhadra and Sudarsana whereas the Patis serve the right side.[6] Further, the seniormost (in age) among the Daitas and Patis becomes the 'chief' (*nayaka*) of both the categories of the temple-servants, i.e., the combined or the joint category of the Daitas and the Patis taken together.[7] Precisely because of this close association of the Daitas and the Patis both the sections or categories of the temple-servants are often wrongly believed — in medieval as well as in modern times — to have belonged to only one section of the temple-servants under the title Daitapatis. But they in fact belong to two different sections or categories of the temple-servants.[8] As Patis are not only the brahmanas but also undoubtedly the priests their non-brahmana counterpart, the Daitas, can also be accorded the priestly or at least the semi-priestly status. In addition to that it should be pointed out here that if the period of impurity (and also the mourning) prescribed by the Hindu scriptures and caused by the birth or death of a kin among the Daitas and the period between the *Snana Yatra* (the bathing-ceremony) and the end of the *Ratha Yatra* (car-festival) overlap, the Daitas do not observe the period of impurity and continue to perform ritual services to the deities including touching the deities[9] which is otherwise a taboo strictly observed by the other temple-servants including the brahmanas. This is significant and very clearly establishes the importance of the Daitas in the hierarchy of the temple-servants. Further, during the *Navakalevara*, i.e., the periodic renewal of the images of the deities, the Daitas are treated as the kins of the deities. To quote Tripathi, "When finally the life-substance of the old Jagannatha statues is transferred into the new ones and the old ones are buried, the Daitas start weeping and crying. They mourn for Jagannatha whom they consider to be one of *their* clan. They remain in the state of ritual impurity for 10 days and take a small frugal meal during this period. They leave their hair unshaved and observe all sorts of obsequies prescribed in the Hindu *Dharmasastras*. On the tenth day they come to the temple, rub oil on their bodies near the *Muktimandapa*, proceed to the Markandeya tank where they let their hair and nails cut and take a purificatory bath in this tank. They also whitewash their houses for which the costs are borne by the Temple. The Temple also supplies foodgrains and vegetable, etc. to them during the state of their ritual impurity. On the 12th day the Daitas give a feast (*mrtyubhoja*) to the servitors of the Temple which they themselves organize and meet the costs of.

Since the heirs of a deceased person inherit his property, the Daitas lay claim on the articles used by the 'deceased' Jagannatha. The Temple, therefore, has to pay some money to the Daitas by way of redemption or compensation (e.g. Rs. 5,000 in 1969). However, they are allowed to take the 'relics' of the old statue like the cloth strips, sandal paste and resin, etc. which they mostly sell to the pilgrims who attach high religious importance to these objects.[10] All these very clearly indicate the priestly or semi-priestly status (or at least very high status) and rank enjoyed by the Daitas in the hierarchy of the temple servants.

The major services of the Sudha Suaras as temple servants include the cleaning of the plates/utensils, collecting materials for the *mangalaropana* rites, making preparation and necessary arrangements for the ritual bath of the deities, cleaning the place of *puja*, i.e., worship before it takes place especially during the car-festival and the *navakalevara* or the periodic renewal of images, breaking the pulses, supplying the paste which is applied to the images before they are painted annually, etc.[11]

Like the Daitas they do not also observe the period of impurity (and mourning) sanctioned by the Hindu scriptures caused by the birth and/or death of a kin if it coincides with the period between the *Snana Yatra* (bathing-ceremony) and the *Ratha Yatra* (car-festival).[12] This again clearly indicates their importance, rank and status in the hierarchy of the temple servants. On the whole they are very high functionaries and can be accorded priestly or semi-priestly status in the cult of Jagannatha.

Now there are reasons to believe that the Daitas and the Sudha Suaras, who are given so much of importance and are accorded very high status (and perhaps priestly or semi-priestly status) in the hierarchy of the temple servants, are almost certainly of tribal origin.

As to the reasons why the Daitas and the Sudha Suaras are believed to be of tribal origin, firstly the temple records like the *Desakhanja* section of the *Madala Panji* as well as a paper manuscript found in the Gopi Tirtha Matha of Bhubaneswar, which is closely related to the former, mention that the Daitas are of tribal origin and the descendants of the original tribal (Savara) worshipper or priest.[13] Further the *Karmangi* of the temple of Jagannatha as well as the Record-of-Rights recognise the Sudha Suaras as a sub-category of the Daita category of the temple servants.[14]

Secondly the tribal origin of the Daitas as well as the Sudha Suaras has been mentioned in *Sarala Mahabharata* and also in *Deula Tola* texts by (Sisu) Krsna Das and Magunia Das while recording the Nila Madhava-Jagannatha tradition. *Sarala Mahabharata* recognizes only two broad categories of the temple servants (or really the priests) of the temple of Jagannatha:

(i) The brahmanas, the descendants of the brahmana explorer Basu (the corresponding Sanskrit form being Vasu or Visva Vasu);[15]

(ii) the Daitas or the non-brahmanas, the descendants of the original Savara worshipper/priest Jara *alias* Basu[16] (the corresponding Sanskrit form for Basu being Vasu or Visva Vasu).

Deula Tola by (Sisu) Krsna Das in contrast mentions three major categories of the temple servants (or again the priests) on the basis of their origin:

(i) The real *sebakas* (servants), i.e., the brahmanas, the descendants of brahmana explorer Bidyapati (the corresponding Sanskrit form being Vidyapati) by his brahmana wife;[17]

(ii) the Daitas or the non-brahmanas, the descendants of the original worshipper-cum-Savara chief Basu (the corresponding Sanskrit form being Vasu or Visva Vasu);[18] and

(iii) the Sudha Suaras, the half-brahmanas or semi-brahmanas, the descendants of brahmana Bidyapati by his Savara wife Lalita, the daughter of the Savara chief Basu.[19]

On the other hand *Deula Tola* by Magunia Das mentions the following three categories of temple servants:

(i) the Daitapatis,

(ii) the Suaras, i.e., the cooks (of Balabhadra *gotra* or clan),

(iii) the Pasupalakas.

According to this text the Daitapatis belong to a single category of temple servants instead of two, i.e., the Daitas and the Patis and are supposed to be descendants of the Savara chief who was worshipping the Nila Madhava in the forest.[20] But this text is silent regarding the progenitors of the other two categories of the temple servants, i.e., the Suaras and the Pasupalakas.

Some other medieval texts like *Bhaba Samudra*, ascribed

to the sixteenth century saint-poet Balaram Das, which is doubtful, *Caitanya Caritamrt*, written in Bengali either in the late sixteenth or in early seventeenth century, and the *Rajabhoga*, section of *Madala Panji* also mention the Daitas.[21] *Bhaba Samudra*, — which, like the *Deula Tola* text by Magunia Das, confuses the Daitas with the Patis and uses the term Daitapati, — mentions their Savara origin. *Caitanya Caritamrt* mentions the Daitas in the context of early sixteenth century, i.e., while describing the car-festival witnessed by Caitanya and recognizes them to be an important category of temple servants or as priest-functionaries playing a certain role in the car-festival in those days as is the custom today. The *Rajabhoga* section of *Madala Panji* mentions the Daitas in an even earlier context, i.e., the pre-Ganga period of Orissan history. According to the *Rajabhoga* the worship of Jagannatha at Puri was discontinued for a period of one hundred and fortyfour years due to the foreign invasion and during that period the images of the deities of the Puri temple had to be kept concealed in a far-off place in western Orissa.[22] Later Jajati Kesari, the founder of the Kesari dynasty, came to the throne of Orissa.[23] He wanted to re-install Lord Jagannatha at Puri and re-start the worship. Therefore he went to western Orissa in search of the images and discovered the same in dilapidated condition. So he wanted to renew the images. For that purpose he invited the Daitas from a place called Biribandha and the Patis from Ratanapur border because of their very important roles in any renewal of the images. At that time he also established some new services for the deities in favour of the tree-cutter brahmanas, the Patis and also the Daitas. But neither *Caitanya Caritamrt* nor the *Rajabhoga* section of *Madala Panji* says anything regarding the origin of the Daitas.

Besides the evidences of the temple records like the *Desakhanja* section of *Madala Panji*, the Gopi Tirtha Matha manuscript, the *Karmangi* and the Record-of-Rights and the medieval Oriya texts like *Sarala Mahabharata, Bhaba Samudra* and the *Deula Tola* texts by (Sisu) Krsna Das and Magunia Das, the names Daita and Sudha Suara lead to the belief that both the Daitas as well as the Sudha Suaras are of tribal origin.

Daita is neither a Hindu caste or *jati* name nor a functional description of that category of priests as is the case with many other temple servants (*sevaka*) including the priests. Though the tribal origin of the Daitas has generally been accepted by the scholars, strangely enough according to some of them like Padhi, Geib and Tripathi the word has been derived from the Sanskrit word *daitya* meaning demon.[24] According to Padhi who has tried to explain this derivation, the terms *daitya, savara* and *bhila* are synonyms or at least these words have been used as synonyms in Sanskrit texts like *Skanda Purana*. In other words the word *daitya* means tribals in general; and the *savara* and the *bhila* being tribal communities it also means the Soras and the Bhils.[25] Thus, Padhi indirectly of course accepts the tribal origin of the Daitas. But let that not divert our attention from the derivation of the word Daita. Though words like Savara and Bhila might have been used as synonyms of the word *daitya* in the later Sanskrit texts like *Skanda Purana*, there is no evidence to the effect that they were so earlier. Further even in later Sanskrit texts and texts in other Indian languages the word *Daitya* is rarely used, if at all, to mean tribals in general or as synonyms to words like *savara* and *bhila*. But normally in Sanskrit and other Indian languages it is used to mean the demon or *raksasa* or *asura*. The *raksasas* or demons have been given this name *daitya* as they are supposed to be sons of Daksa Prajapati's daughter Diti, according to the Indian mythology.[26] So, it is highly unlikely that on the basis of this rarely used, if ever, sense of the term *daitya* a section of priests of Jagannatha, who were of tribal origin, either called themselves or accepted when others called them *daita* or *daitya*, which otherwise, and commonly, was used to mean *raksasa* or demon and therefore, was derogatory, undignified, insulting and unacceptable. It follows that though the derivation of the word Daita from the Sanskrit word *daitya* may support the view that the Daitas are of tribal origin there is a very serious objection to accept that derivation. In that connection it should also be pointed out here that in the Hindu mythological texts Visnu is called Daityari (= *daitya* + *ari*), i.e., the foe or enemy of the *daityas* or demons and *daitya-nasana* or *daitya-nisudana*, i.e., the destroyer or killer of the *daityas* or demons.[27] Therefore, Lord Jagannatha who is identified with Visnu is also the foe or enemy of the *daityas* and the destroyer of the *daityas* or demons. Then how could a section of the priests possibly be called *daityas*, from which the derivation of the word *daita* has been claimed, reducing them to the status of the foe or enemy of Lord Jagannatha. On the whole this derivation is not at all acceptable.

According to K.C. Mishra the word *daita* has been derived from the Sanskrit word *dayita* meaning beloved, dear, cherished as the Daitas, according to him, are very dear to Lord Jagannatha.[28] But this explanation is rather far-fetched. Even if a category of priests declared themselves to be very dear to Lord Jagannatha and labelled themselves accordingly, it is quite unlikely that the other priests ever accepted their superiority and also accepted this label. Again Mishra has not even tried to explain why this section of priests used the rarely used word *dayita* instead of commonly used words like *priya* with the identical meaning. Therefore, this derivation, too, cannot be accepted.

Panigrahi on the other hand prefers the name Daitapati instead of Daita for a section of temple priests. According to him the term Daitapati has been derived from the Sanskrit expression *devata-pati* meaning the custodian of the deity as the word *devata* means god, deity, etc., and the word *pati* means master, custodian, etc.[29] Panigrahi confuses the Patis or Pati Mahapatras, another category of temple priests, with the Daitas and believes that both the Daitas and the Patis or Pati Mahapatras belong to the same category of temple priests to which the name Daitapati has been assigned. But in fact the Daitas and the Patis or Pati Mahapatras are *sevakas* or priests of two completely different categories though they are often confused as a single category.[30] Furthermore the Pati Mahapatras are considered to be brahmanas whereas the Daitas are considered to be of tribal origin.[31] Other brahmanas of lower category with *devata* as surname or family name are found in Orissa. But the Daitas of the temple of Jagannatha at Puri have nothing to do with them and have Swain and Das as surnames or family names and Mahapatra as title. Therefore, the Daitas and persons with *devata* surname/family name cannot be equated.

It is really strange that most of these scholars while accepting the tribal origin of the Daitas have invariably tried to derive the name from Sanskritic or Āryan sources. Instead of trying to trace the origin of the word Daita from one of such Sanskrit sources which is far-fetched it may be accepted as a word of Austroasiatic or Munda origin as the Daitas are supposed to be of Savara origin who may be identified with the Savara hill tribe of the Ganjam and Vizagapatam tract speaking an Austroasiatic tongue. Another reason for tracing the origin of the word Daita to an Austroasiatic language spoken by the Savara or Sora hill tribe of the Ganjam and Vizagapatam tract through the Savara forefathers of the Daitas — which is claimed by the traditional account — is linked with the identification of the Sudha Suara category of the temple servants, who are supposedly of Daita origin, with a sub-class of the Savaras or Soras which is quite likely as will be evident shortly. Most probably this word Daita or the original Austroasiatic word from which it has been derived (which is not known at present) originally denoted a particular class or sub-class of the Savara or Sora tribals who used to worship the pre-Hinduized Lord Jagannatha.

Similarly scholars like Mishra, Geib, Tripathi ,etc. have — either directly or indirectly — derived the expression Sudha

Suara from the Sanskrit words *suddha*, meaning pure or holy and *supakara* (from *supa* meaning sauce/broth/soup), meaning cook[32] and assumed that the compound word means the holy temple cook. But contrary to the assumption of these scholars the Sudha Suaras do not perform any cooking service in the temple as has already been mentioned. The cooking is done by cooks of several different categories also known as the Suaras, which word, of course, has been derived from the Sanskrit word, *supakara*. It appears that as the cooks are also known as the Suaras it confused the above-mentioned scholars and misled them to derive the expression Sudha Suara from the Sanskrit words *suddha* and *supakara* meaning the holy temple cook. Therefore, it seems that the Sudha Suaras are not 'the holy temple cooks' or Suddha Supakaras as has been assumed.

E. Thruston, back in 1909, observed eight sub-classes among the Savara or Saura or Sora hill tribe of Ganjam and Vizagapatam tract, i.e., present south Orissa and north Andhra Pradesh which were grouped under two major classes as follows:[33]

A. *Hill Savaras*

i. Savara, Jati Savara (Savaras *par excellence*) or Maliah Savara
ii. Arsi, Arisi or Lombo Lanjiya
iii. Luara or Muli
iv. Kindal
v. Jadu
vi. Kumbi

B. *Savaras of the low country*

vii. Kapu or Pallapu/Kudung or Besang
viii. Sudho

As Lord Jagannatha is known to be a Hinduized tribal deity it is quite likely that some of his priests may also be of tribal origin which is even claimed by some of the versions of Nila Madhava-Jagannatha tradition as well as the temple records. Therefore, the Sudha Suaras, a category of the temple-servants with either priestly or semi-priestly status, may be connected with the Sudhos or Sudhas which is one of eight sub-classes of the Savara or Saura or Sora hill tribe of Ganjam and Vizagapatam tract. That will explain the *sudha* part of the name Sudha Suara. Thruston of course claims that the name Sudho means pure.[34] In other words he believes that the term Sudho has been derived from the Sanskrit word *Suddha* meaning pure. But this view of Thruston cannot be accepted as he has not tried to derive the other seven names from the Sanskritic sources.[35] If the other names are not of Sanskritic origin then why Thruston considers the name of only one of the sub-classes of Savaras or Soras as of Sanskritic origin? It seems that only the similarity in the pronunciation of both the words — the name of one of the sub-classes of the Savara hill tribe and the Sanskrit word *suddha*—has led him to believe that one word has been derived from the other. Instead the word Sudho, the name of one of the sub-classes of the Savaras, might have been derived from one of the following three homonym morphemes:

(i) sUd-(to transfer grain etc. into basket with one's own hand, to give)

(ii) sUd-(to drench, to make wet)

(iii) sUd-(to spread all around)

or the word:

sUda-(large, big, great)

found in Sora language[36] or words related to one of these morphemes or the word, sUda.

Similarly the 'Suara' part of the name Sudha Suara might have been derived from the word 'Saura' now current in Orissa to denote the Savara or Sora hill tribe as per the principle of sound change called metathesis.[37] (The word Saura, in turn, might have been derived from the Sanskrit word *savara*. It may also be that the word *savara* is the Sanskritized form of the word Saura or some such word.) In that case the word *suara* has no genetic relationship with the Sanskrit word *supakara* meaning cook. This is further corroborated by the fact that the Sudha Suaras do not do any cooking service in the temple as has been explained earlier. Therefore, it will be quite reasonable to suppose that the Sudha Suaras are of Savara — especially of the Sudha sub-class of the same — origin.

An examination of the following facts will only corroborate the above inference. It should be noted that a sizeable number of the inhabitants of the district of Puri in Orissa belong to a caste or *jati* called Sudha. According to O'Malley, who depending on the 1901 census data, wrote in 1908, the Sudhas were occupying numerically the fifth place among the *jati*s of the district of Puri, — coming after the Chasas, the brahmanas, the Bauris and the Gauras in that order, — numbering 41,080 out of a total population of 1,017,284.[38] According to the 1911 census the number of the Sudhas in the district of Puri was 42,950[39] out of a total population of 1,023,402.[40] In the same year the number of the total population of the Sudhas in Orissa was 79,334.[41] According to the Puri District Gazetteer of 1929 the Sudhas continued to retain the numerically fifth position among the different *jati*s in the district of Puri numbering 40,443 out of the total population of 951,661 which was based on the 1921 census data.[42] Further these Sudhas of the district of Puri are considered to be of tribal origin or really aborigines.[43] (Of course nowadays many Sudhas of the district of Puri claim to be of ksatriya or Khandayata and some to be of Karana caste or *jati*.) Besides the Sudhas, the Savaras and the Sahars, who are clearly of Saura or Sora origin, are also found in the District of Puri.[44]

Apart from the Sudhas, the Savaras and the Sahars other aboriginal people are also found in the district of Puri. O'Malley, in 1908, observed, "A large proportion of the population still consists of aboriginal races or semi-Hinduized castes, such as

Bauris who number 84,188, Sahars (18,095), Pans (7,064), Savars (3,260), and Khonds (2,560). . . . Every village in Khurda where these aborigines dwell has its Bauri and Savar quarter."[45] According to 1971 and 1981 censuses the scheduled tribes form 3.70 and 3.45 per cent respectively of the total population of the district of Puri.[46] Besides that the scheduled castes forming 13.53 and 12.93 per cent respectively of the total population of the district[47] are mainly of tribal origin. It may be noted that in the census records the Sudhas figure under neither of the groups, i.e., neither under the scheduled tribes nor under the scheduled castes. Therefore, if the percentage of the Sudha population is added to the scheduled tribe population the total percentage of their population to the total population will rise even further. Again the Bauris and Pans whom O' Malley considers as aboriginals, meanwhile have come under the scheduled castes in the census records. (The above facts along with the fact that nowadays many of the Sudhas of the district of Puri claim to be of ksatriya or Khandayata or Karana caste or *jati* clearly indicate how otherwise the tribal absorption and *jati* mobility processes have been in operation in that region.)

In that connection it may be mentioned here that a sizeable number of Sudhas are also found in other parts of Orissa especially in the western part and even beyond the western border of Orissa.[48] Though these Sudhas are also believed to be of tribal origin they do not claim any Saura or Savara affiliation.

The facts presented above can be explained in the following manner. Once upon a time the area comprising the present district of Puri including areas in and about the Puri town was largely inhabited by the aborigines or the autochthonous tribes and among them figured a sizeable number of the Sauras or Savaras, speakers of an Austroasiatic language, and especially the Sudha section of the same. Later with the advent of the Aryans most probably some of them retreated and/or were pushed into the interior hills or forests inhabited by their fellow tribes, both in the west and in the south, but others continued to inhabit the area either as aborigines or gradually getting absorbed into the Hindu society. Generally the Sudhas of the south continued to retain their Austroasiatic tongue as well as their Saura or Savara affiliation—perhaps because of the concentration and dominant position of the Sauras there—whereas the Sudhas of the west and of the district of Puri in course of time — while gradually getting absorbed into the Hindu society — forgot their own Austroasiatic language, substituting it by another especially of Aryan derivation, and also their Saura affiliation. This explains why most of the speakers of the Austroasiatic Saura or Savara language, in fact more than 95 per cent of them, are to be found only in south Orissa (i.e., the Ganjam and Koraput districts) and north Andhra Pradesh.

If the picture painted above — which appears to be quite plausible—is accepted then the Sudhas of the district of Puri can be connected on one hand with the Sudhas of the south, i.e., one of the eight sub-classes of the Savara or Saura hill tribe found in the Ganjam and Vizagapatam tract as well as with the Sudhas of the west, found in the western part and even beyond the western border of Orissa, and on the other with the Sudha Suaras, a category of temple-servants of the Jagannatha temple, Puri with either the priestly or semi-priestly status, providing a link between the former and the latter.

From the above discussion it is now clear that the Sudha Suaras, a category of the temple-servants of the Jagannatha temple at Puri, are most probably of Saura or Savara — and especially of the Sudho or Sudha sub-class — origin. This inference is further strengthened by the fact that according to O' Malley the tutelary deity of the Sudhas of the district of Puri is goddess Khambesvari.[49] This Hinduized, tribal deity, 'the lady of the post', also called Stambhesvari, 'the lady of the pillar', perhaps a Sanskritized form of the former, is very closely associated with the emergence and evolution of the cult of

Jagannatha providing a strong connecting link in the long-drawn-out process of Hinduization of that pre-Hinduized tribal deity as has been pointed out very clearly by Anncharlott Eschmann and others.[50] In that conncetion Eschmann observes, "As the worship of Khambesvari is known since the fifth century AD her Hinduized iconography might be taken as the proto-type for the development which led to the Subhadra figure", [51] and Kulke also says, ". . . Stambhesvari ('goddess of the pillar') cult which had — especially iconographically — a strong correspondence with the Subhadra and the Sudarsana images of the Jagannatha triad."[52] It has also further been observed, "Both, the figures of Khambesvari and of Jagannatha developed from the same tribal substrata. It could be shown that these types of tribal cults must have in pre-Yayati times been present on the seashore."[53] All these observations are of crucial importance to our thesis here. Therefore, it may safely be concluded that the Sudha Suaras of the Puri temple are of Sudha Saura origin.

To sum up so far no satisfactory Sanskritic source for the derivation of the names — either Daita or Sudha Suara — has been found. On the other hand a highly satisfactory alternative tribal (i.e., Austroasiatic) source for the derivation of the name Sudha Suara has been discovered. Therefore, the tribal, i.e., Saura or Savara origin of the Sudha Suaras (as well as of the Daitas, who are supposed to have been very closely related to the Sudha Suaras) may be inferred which supports the earlier mentioned evidence of the temple records like the *Desakhanja* section of *Madala Panji*, the *Karmangi* and the Record-of-Rights as well as of *Sarala Mahabharata* and the *Deula Tola* texts by Sisu Krsna Das and Magunia Das.[54]

Further it appears that the Daita category of the temple-servants are not only of Saura or Savara origin like the Sudha Suaras, the other category of temple-servants but most probably originally belonged to a sub-class of the Sudha Sauras (i.e. Sudha Savaras/Soras) which also included the Sudha Suaras. This conclusion has been arrived at on the basis of the following reasoning. As has been mentioned earlier the temple records like the *Karmangi* and the Record-of- Rights very clearly mention that the Sudha Suaras really belong to the Daita category of the temple-servants which is quite significant in this connection.[55] It should further be pointed out that the *Deula Tola* version of the Nila Madhava-Jagannatha tradition, the only version that mentions the Sudha Suaras, also admits blood-relationship between these two categories of temple-servants. Again it was highly unlikely for two completely separate aboriginal tribes to worship the same tribal deity, later to be Hinduized and ultimately became Lord Jagannatha of today, as their own deity which also leads to the conclusion that the Daitas and the Sudha Suaras originally belonged to one and the same tribe. Finally the earlier *Sarala Mahabharata* edition of the Nila Madhava-Jagannatha tradition mentions only the Daitas but is silent about the Sudha Suaras whereas the *Deula Tola* text by Sisu Krsna Das, the later version of the tradition, mentions both the Daitas and the Sudha Suaras as major categories of priest-functionaries of Lord Jagannatha. There is a time-gap of several hundred years between the date of earlier *Sarala Mahabharata* and later *Deula Tola* versions of the tradition. The earliest reference to the Sudha Suaras is found in the *Karmangi* which was perhaps written at the end of the sixteenth century, about one hundred and fifty years after *Sarala Mahabharata* was written. Taking all these facts into consideration one tends to further conclude that the Sudha Suaras emerged as a separate major category of priest-functionaries only later, at least a hundred and fifty years after Sarala *Mahabharata* was written.

To sum up earlier — i.e., before their emergence as a separate major category of priest-functionaries — the Sudha Suaras were included in the Daita category of the priest-functionaries (and were at best a sub-category of the same). Therefore, whenever the term Daita occurred in the earlier contexts, especially in *Sarala*

Mahabharata, it was inclusive of that sub-category or sub-group of priest-functionaries which was later to emerge as a separate major category of priest-functionaries called the Sudha Suaras. The name Sudha Suara was assumed by them when they emerged as a separate major category of priest-functionaries in order to establish their separate and independent identity from the Daita category.

If a sub-category of the Daita category of the priest-functionaries emerged as a separate category at a later period and in order to establish and emphasize their separate and independent identity assumed the name Sudha Suara then it can be argued that the Daitas themselves belonged to the Sudha sub-class of the Sauras or Savaras originally. Otherwise why a sub-category of the Daitas assumed the name Sudha Suara, most probably derived from the expression Sudha Saura, for themselves in their search for an independent identity? Therefore, it may be concluded that the Daitas originally belonged to the Sudha sub-class of the Sauras or Savaras and precisely for that reason a sub-category of the Daita category of the priest-functionaries, when seeking a separate and independent identity for themselves, preferred to assume the original tribal group name as the name of their group or category. It appears that they had certainly forgotten their Saura/Savara affiliation, but not completely by that time (i.e., the time of their emergence as a separate major category of priest-functionaries). At least the changed name Sudha Suara (derived from the original name Sudha Saura) was there in the collective memory of the group or class however indistinct or faint that might have become over the years.

The following diagram seeks to show the hypothetical genetic relationship existing among the Sauras/Savaras/Soras, the Sudhas/Sudhos (a sub-section of the Sauras/Savaras/Soras), the Daitas (a category of priests of the temple of Jagannatha at Puri) and the Sudha Suaras (another category of priests of the temple of Jagannatha):

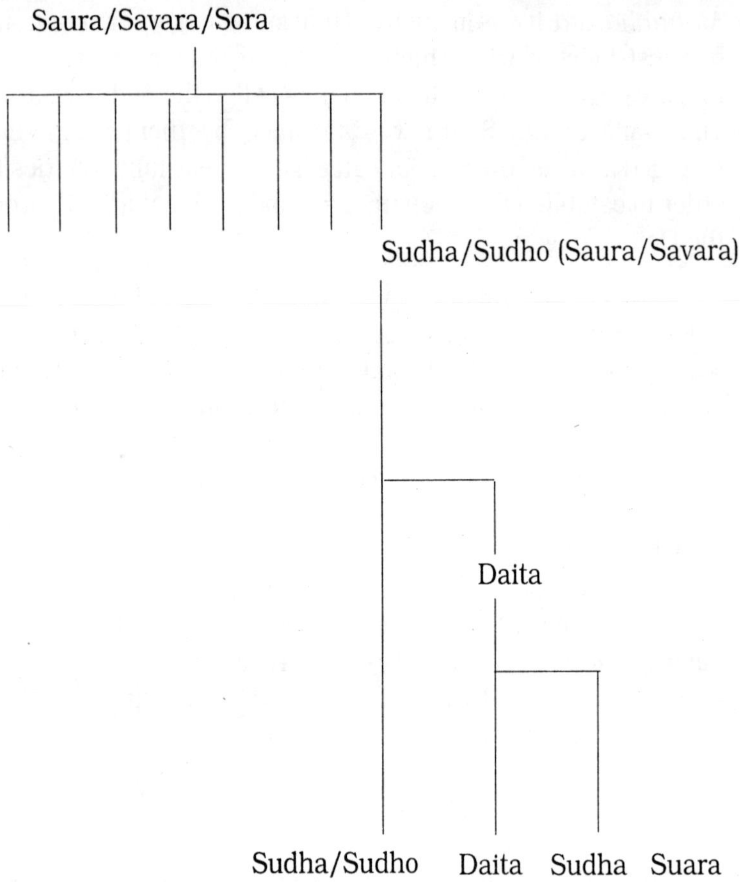

An important corollary of the above discussion is that the term Savara occurring in the different versions of the Nila Madhava-Jagannatha tradition could not have been used as a generic term meaning just any aboriginal tribe as some scholars have assumed but only as a specific term to denote the Sudha sub-class of the Saura or Savara hill tribe speaking an Austroasiatic language of which again the Daitas were a sub-class. In other words the Sudha sub-class of the Saura or Savara hill tribe were the original worshippers of a tribal deity which in course of time got Hinduized and ultimately became Lord Jagannatha of today. To phrase it differently the pre-Hinduized or tribal substrata of Lord Jagannatha was the tutelary deity (*ista devata*) of the Sudha sub-class of the Savara or Saura or Sora hill tribe, speakers of an Austroasiatic language, which inhabited the area in and about Puri town in distant past. With the advent of the Aryans to the region some of them retreated southward and some westward but others remained in that area. Again some of them who remained retained their tribal/aboriginal way of life but many got gradually Hinduized. Of the latter some got Hinduized through the Hinduization of the tribal deity they worshipped because of their very close association with the same but others otherwise. The Daitas and the Sudha Suaras are the Hinduized descendants of some of the original Sudha priests of the pre-Hinduized Lord Jagannatha who got Hinduized through their close association with that deity.

A second important corollary of the above discussion is that the deity Khambesvari or 'the lady of the post' was not brought to Puri from western Orissa, her only and real homeland, in order to be united with another local tribal deity — resulting in the emergence of the Hindu goddess Subhadra when her companion deity was Hinduized and became Lord Jagannatha as has sometimes been assumed. On the contrary Puri was also very much the homeland of 'the lady of the post', a tutelary deity of the Sudha sub-section of the Suara or Savara hill tribe inhabiting the area. The Hinduization and consequent transformation of this deity took several different directions. While one such direction led to the emergence of the semi-Hinduized deity Khambesvari, a different direction united 'the lady of the post' with another local tribal deity which ultimately resulted in the emergence of the Hindu goddess Subhadra, when her companion deity was also Hinduized and became Lord Jagannatha of the famous Puri triad.

Notes

1. For more information on this theory ***see*** Padhi, 1975; Geib,

1975; Mishra, K.C., 1971.

2. Geib, 1975: 131, 180.
3. Kulke, 1978a: 130-31.
4. Record-of-Rights, Part III (iii), Vol. 1, Gazette No. 293, 1955: 7-10.
5. For more information ***see*** Singh, J., 1964: 518-19; Record-of-Rights, Part III (iii), Vol. 2, *Seba* No. 20: 178-200 and also Part II, Gazette No. 101, 1955: 57-82; *Desakhanja* ORP: 181-85; Gopi Tirtha Matha MSS, ORP: 178-83; *Karmangi*, 1983: 142-44. *Karmangi*, according to the preface in the text itself (1983: 107), has been compiled during the reign of one Ramachandra Dev, who can be identified with Ramachandra I (1568-1600) of the second Bhoi dynasty. ***See*** also Mahapatra, C., 1969: 382 which, of course, is not very authentic or reliable as it seems to have been edited and in the process has been considerably altered at a later period.
6. Singh, J., 1964: 518; *Desakhanja*, ORP: 181-82; Gopi Tirtha Matha MSS, ORP: 178-79.
7. *Ibid.*
8. As for example in *Deula Tola* by Magunia Das, a medieval text, the Daitas and the Patis have been treated as a single category/group of temple servants under the caption Daitapati. ***See*** *Deula Tola*, K. C. Sahu MSS: folio 87a (5/56). This is also the case with another medieval text named *Bhaba Samudra* ascribed to the sixteenth century saint-poet Balaram Das which is doubtful. ***See*** *Bhaba Samudra*, 1910: 47-48. In modern times K.C. Mishra and K.C. Panigrahi also believe that the Daitas and the Patis belong to a single category/group of temple servants which is called the Daitapati. ***See*** Mishra, 1971: 95 and Panigrahi, 1981: 340. But this is erroneous. The Daitas and the Patis belong to two different categories/groups of the temple servants. In the Record-of-Rights, Part III (iii) the Daitas belong to the group/category doing the *Seba* No. 20 and the Patis belong to another group/category doing the *Seba* No. 21 among the hundred and odd groups/categories of temple servants. The *Rajabhoga* section of *Madala Panji*, *Karmangi*, *Desakhanja* and Gopi Tirtha Matha MSS treat them as two

different groups/categories of temple servants and so does J. Singh in modern times.

9. *Desakhanja*, ORP: 182; Gopi Tirtha Matha MSS, ORP: 180. The period between the *Snana Yatra* and *Ratha Yatra* is known as Anasara (from Sk. *Anavasara*) and during this period the deities remain within the Anasara enclosure.

10. Tripathi, G.C., 1978: 261.

11. Record-of-Rights, Part III (iii), Vol. 4, Gazette No. 203, 1956: 10-19. **See** also *Desakhanja*, ORP: 207-09; Gopi Tirtha Matha MSS, ORP: 202-04 and *Karmangi*, 1983: 128-29. Of course according to *Desakhanja* and Gopi Tirtha Matha MSS the Sudha Suara selects and washes the different seasonal fruits to be offered as food (*bhoga*) to the deities and dresses the same for the purpose. But he is never involved in real cooking.

12. Record-of-Rights, Part III (iii), Vol. 4, *Seba* No. 37, Gazette No. 203, 1956: 12.

13. *Desakhanja*, ORP: 181; Gopi Tirtha Matha MSS, ORP: 178.

14. *Karmangi*, 1983: 128; Record-of-Rights, Part III (iii), Vol. 4, *Seba* No. 37, 1956: 19.

15. *basu brāhmaṇa baṃśa karibāka pūjā/*

    yeheneka prastāba bākya māgilā indradyumna rājā//

    —*Sarala Mahabharata, Musali Parba*, (12/153): 117

    Translation : The king Indradyumna asked the favour that the descendants of brahmana Basu would do the act of worshipping, i.e., they will be the priests.

16. *jāhā se sarjanā kalā deba dhātā/*

    jārā śabara baṃśa hoile daitā//

    —*Sarala Mahabharata, Musali Parba*, (12/151): 117

    Translation : This is what god Brahma had ordained that the descendants of the Savara Jara became the Daitas.

17.(a) *bidyāpati brāhmaṇara putra hele jāta/*

prakṛta sebaka sehi hoibe re suta//

—*Deula Tola* by (Sisu) Krsna Das, Kohinoor Press

edition, 1953: 20 and also Prabhati Pustakalaya edition: 19.

Translation : If a son would be born to the brahmana Bidyapati then he (that son) would be the real servant (of Lord Jagannatha).

(b) *jeũ brāhmaṇa tohara dūta paṇe galā/*
nīḷa mādhaba rūpa bheṭa se pāilā//
se brāhmaṇa ghare jeũ putra heba jāta/
prakr̥ta sebaka se bolibe jagannātha//

— *Deula Tola* by (Sisu) Krsna Das, Dasarathi Pustakalaya edition, 1950: 25.

Translation : Lord Jagannatha would say that the son that would be born in the house (i.e., the family) of the brahmana who went as your messenger (i.e., explorer) and who discovered the image of Nila Madhava he would be the real servant (of Lord Jagannatha).

18.(a) *mo aṅga sebaka basu āḷe heba suta/*
daitā sebaka sehi hebare nr̥nātha//

— *Deula Tolą* by (Sisu) Krsna Das, Kohinoor Press edition, 1953: 19-20.

(b) *mo aṅga sebaka basu āḷe heba suta/*
daitā sebaka sehi heba nr̥panātha//

— *Deula Tola* by (Sisu) Krsna Das, Prabhati Pustakalaya edition: 19.

Translation of (a) and (b) : O king! the son born to (Savara) Basu, the servant of my body (i.e., my servant) will be the Daita servant.

(c) *jebaṇa śabara goṭi banastare thilā/*
nīḷa je mādhaba rūpa āmbhara pūjilā//
śabarara ghare jeũ putra hebe jāta/
daitā sebaka hebe bole jagannātha//

— *Deula Tola* by (Sisu) Krsna Das, Dasarathi Pustakalaya edition, 1950: 25.

Translation : Lord Jagannatha said that the son that would be born in the house (i.e., family) of the Savara who was (residing) in the forest and who worshipped my Nila Madhava image/ form he (i.e., the son) would be the Daita servant (*sevaka*).

19.(a) *laḷitā aurasu śuṇa putra jāta hele/*

śuddha suāra hoiba śrī hari boile//

— *Deula Tola* by (Sisu) Krsna Das, Kohinoor Press edition, 1953: 20 and Prabhati Pustakalaya edition: 19.

Translati on: Sri Hari said that the son that would be born to Lalita (the Savara girl who was married to brahmana) would be Sudha Suara (servant).

(b) *bidyāpati brāhmaṇa je dūta paṇe galā/*

śabara jhiaku se je pradāna hoilā//

śabaruṇī ṭhāru jeũ putra heba jāta/

śuddha suāra se hebe bole jagannātha//

— *Deula Tola* by (Sisu) Krsna Das, Dasarathi Pustakalaya edition, 1950: 26

Translation : Brahmana Bidyapati went as an explorer and was married to the Savara girl. Lord Jagannatha said that the son that would be born to this Savara woman would be the Suddha Suara.

20. *jeũ śabara bane thilā/*

nīḷa mādheba pūju thilā// (5/54)

je putra tāra jāta heba/

se putra sebaka hoiba// (5/55)

daitāpati nāma tāra/

sebaka hoiba āmbhara// (5/56)

suāra baḷabhadra gotrī/

karibe : folio 87a

roṣa panti panti// (5/57)

pasupāḷaka daitāpati/

karibe pūjā bidhi nīti// (5/58) : folio 87b

—*Deula Tola* by Magunia Das, K.C. Sahu MSS.

Translation : (Bhabagrahi, i.e., Lord Jagannatha said) "The son that will be born to the Savara, who was living in the forest and was worshipping Nila Madhava, will be the servant (of the Lord). His name is Daitapati; he will be our servant. The cooks (suara) belonging to the clan (*gotra*) of Balabhadra will do different kinds/varieties of cooking. The Pasupalakas and the Daitapatis will do the worshipping as per the prescribed rules.

See note no. 8 in this connection.

21.(a) *Bhaba Samudra*, 1910: 47-48 (stanzas 125-26). **See** note no. 8 in this connection.

(b) *Caitanya Caritamrt*, Madhya, 13/7-9.

(c) *Madala Panji*, 1940: 5-6.

22. K.C. Panigrahi identifies the foreign invasion mentioned in the *Rajabhoga* section of *Madala Panji* with the Rastrakuta invasion of Orissa either in the late eighth or in early ninth century. Panigrahi, 1981: 78-79. **See** also Panigrahi, 1961: 26-27.

23. K.C. Panigrahi identifies this Jajati Kesari of the *Rajabhoga* section of *Madala Panji* with Yayati I of the Somavamsi kings. **See** Panigrahi, 1961: 26-27, 32-33 and 1981: 79, 105-06. H. von Stietencron tends to agree with him. **See** Stietencron, 1978a: 17. But Kulke identifies this Jajati Kesari with Yayati II of the Somavamsi kings. **See** Kulke, 1978b: 141-44.

24.(a) Padhi, 1975: 25.

(b) Geib, 1975: 191.

(c) Tripathi, G.C., 1978: 224.

25. Padhi, 1975: 25.

26. **See** *A Sanskrit-English Dictionary* by Monier Monier-Williams and *Encyclopaedia of Religion and Ethics*, Vol. 4 under the entry 'Daitya' by Hermann Jacobi.

27. **See** *A Sanskrit-English Dictionary* by Monier Monier-Williams.

28. Mishra, K.C., 1971: 95.

29. Panigrahi, 1981: 340.

30. **See** note no. 8.

31. **See** notes no. 5 and 8.

32. Mishra, 1971: 82; Geib, 1975: 165, 170; Tripathi, G.C., 1978: 225 fn. No. 5. Jakob Rosel though does not trace the origin of the expression Sudha Suara to Sanskrit Suddha Supakara treats the Sudha Suaras under the category of cooks and renders the term 'Nekterkoche' as the German equivalent of the term Sudha Suara. **See** Rosel, 1980: 54.

33. **See** Thruston, Vol. 6, 1975: 304-05, 308 and 405 for more information. According to Thruston a Hindu caste named Suddha originating out of the Soras later got absorbed into the Hindu society. **See** also Choudhury, 1963-64: 101-02.

34. Thruston, Vol. 6, 1975: 308, 405.

35. *Ibid.*, 304-05.

36. **See** Ramamurti, 1938: 263.

37. According to Hockett, "Metathesis replaces an old form by a new one which differs in that two parts have been interchanged: disintregation for disintegration, . . ." Hockett, 1970: 391. According to Lehmann, "By Metathesis we mean interchange of phonemes." Lehmann, 1975: 169.

38. O'Malley, 1908: 79.

39. Census of India, 1911, Vol. 5, Bihar and Orissa, Part III, Tables by L.S.S. O'Malley.

40. O'Malley, 1929: 63.

41. Census of India, 1911, Vol. 5, Bihar and Orissa, Part III.

42. O'Malley, 1929: 87.

43. O'Malley, 1908: 82.

44. O'Malley, 1908: 71-72; 1929: 78.

45. O'Malley, 1908: 71-72.

46. Tripathi, B., 1973: 307 and Swain, S.K., 1989: 122.

47. Tripathi, B., 1973: 306 and Swain, S.K., 1989: 120.

48. **See** Russell and Lal, 1975: 514-16. Eschmann has observed the Sudhas in several places in Orissa like places near Angul, Talcher, Phulbani and Sonepur etc. **See** Eschmann, 1978a: 86, 95; 1978c: 271, 275-77. Chakradhar Mahapatra has observed

the Sudhas in Narsinghpur in the district of Cuttack. ***See*** Mahapatra, C., 1982: 260. ***See*** also Risley 1981: 267-68.

49. ***See*** O'Malley, 1908: 82. D.C. Konar in the District Gazetteers of Puri also observes, "The Sudhas or Suds are mostly found in Ranpur, Nayagarh, Dasapalla, Khandapara and the Khurda area of the district. Agriculture is their principal occupation. They believe that in the days of yore their ancestors were working as soldiers. They worship a deity called Pancha Khanda, i.e. of the five swords, with offerings of goats and fowls, and their tutelary goddess is Khambeswari, represented in the form of a wooden pole (khamba). The Sudhas are divided into four subclasses, (i) the Bara or high Sudha, (ii) the Dehri or worshippers, (iii) the Kabat-Konia and (iv) the Butka. Among them the Bara Sudhas, rank highest." Kunar, D.C., 1977: 137.

50. ***See*** Eschmann, 1978a: 86-87, 92-94; 1978b: 110-11; 1978c: 275-80 and Kulke, H., 1978a: 130; 1978b: 142 and Eschmann *et al.*, 1978: 177-78, 181-82, 195.

51. Eschmann, 1978a: 94.

52. Kulke, H., 1978b: 142.

53. Eschmann *et al.*, 1978: 177-78.

54. ***See*** notes no. 13, 14, 16, 18, 19 and 20.

55. ***See*** note no. 14.

6

Upward Mobility of the Non-Brahmana Priests and the Traditional Account

THE process of absorption and upward mobility in the Hindu society of a category of priests of tribal origin of the Hinduized tribal deity, ultimately known as Lord Jagannatha, and the role of the origin myth in this process can now be studied a little more closely on the basis of the following conclusions drawn in the previous chapter:

(a) the Sudha Suaras, a category of the priests of the Hinduized tribal deity Lord Jagannātha originally belonged to the Daita category of priests, i.e., were a sub-category of the Daitas but later got separated from them and claimed independent identity for themselves.

(b) the Daitas, a major category of the same deity, are the descendants of the original tribal worshippers/priests— who belonged to the Sudha/Sudho branch or sub-class of the Savaras/Sauras (i.e. the Sora hill tribe) speaking an Austroasiatic language—of the tribal deity later to the Hinduized and become Lord Jagannatha of today.

As has already been mentioned, with the Hinduization of the deity the brahmana priests were engaged in order to carry on the worship as per the Brahmanic scriptures. But most probably the rights and privileges of the Daitas simply could not be completely ignored or rejected when the deity got Hinduized and had to be recognised and accepted. Thus they and their descendants were accorded priestly or semi-priestly status in this newly Hinduized cult which initiated the process of their final absorption into the Hindu society. Further with the Hinduization of the deity a mythical traditional account or *mahatmya* centring round the deity also gradually took shape as in the case of the most of the Hindu deities (in fact this is perhaps true in the case of most of the deities/religious shrines in most of the religions). That is how the Nila Madhava-Jagannatha tradition came into being or originated.

Though the process of absorption of the Daitas into the Hindu society started quite early, at the latest by the end of the eleventh century, by which time the tribal deity was to some extent Hinduized,[1] the process was not yet completed and the tribal or the Sora origin of the Daitas was not at all forgotten by the fifteenth century as the *Sarala Mahabharata* version of the Nila Madhava -Jagannatha tradition testifies. Perhaps the brahmanas accorded them the priestly or at least the semi-priestly status rather reluctantly and grudgingly in the first place and always continued to remind everybody, including the Daitas, their (the Daitas') tribal or Sora origin and constantly looked down upon them for that. It must be remembered here that originally there was Brahmanic opposition to the Hinduization of the deity and the cult as reflected in the *Skanda Purana*.[2] Therefore, there was nothing strange in this reluctance or even opposition. It may be that the Daitas themselves did not want the people to forget their tribal or Sora origin lest their rights and privileges to worship the Hinduized tribal deity, Purusottama-Jagannatha, as descendants of the original tribal priest(s) are taken away. Either because of the opposition and hostile attitude of the brahmana priests, who were, after all their rivals and fellow competitors in the priestly profession or because of the ambivalent attitudes of the Daitas themselves, mentioned above, they (the Daitas) could not be completely absorbed into the Hindu society by the fifteenth century.

But with the increasing Hinduization (Brahmanization) of the cult, the power and the prestige of the Daitas, the non-brahmana priests who were not adept in the Brahmanical rituals and rules of purity, etc. suffered and their position was downgraded considerably *vis-a-vis* that of the brahmana priests whose power and prestige increased and position was elevated. A time came when the Daitas felt ignored or even threatened. As a reaction they tried to resist this trend and to protect or even strengthen their power, prestige and position in the cult as well as in the Hindu community of Orissa. It must be very clearly pointed out here that the higher status and the position in the cult (i.e., among the priests) and in the society in real terms meant attracting more pilgrims and collecting a higher fee from them. Both the social status and the monetary gain which accompanied the former were the real driving forces behind the effort of the Daitas to elevate their position. With that end in view they made addition and alterations in the earlier existing traditional account transforming the same into their origin myth and restructuring that in such a way that the superiority of the Daitas over the brahmana priests was established and Lord Jagannatha was made to play the role of supporter and protector of the Daitas or non-brahmana priests in these origin myths.

The *Sarala Mahabharata* version of the Nila Madhava-Jagannatha tradition is an example of such modified and restructured origin myth. It has already been pointed out how it sought to establish the Daitas as the descendants of the original tribal priest, Savara Jara. It was perhaps not completely wrong or false on their part to trace their descendance from the original tribal or Sora priest(s) of the pre-Hinduized tribal deity at Puri. But it is significant that in earlier and Sanskritic (or Brahmanic) version of the tradition this fact was ignored.

Further the *Sarala Mahabharata* version of the tradition

also sought to establish the superiority of the Daitas or the non-brahmana priests in terms of Lord Jagannatha's preference for them in the account of securing the holy log (*daru*). According to this account when king Indradyumna noticed the *daru* in the 'Rohini Kunda' he engaged people to lift it out of the *Kunda*. But the *daru* was so heavy that they were unsuccessful. Indradyumna was at a loss and did not know what to do. Then the Lord told him in a dream that only Savara Jara and brahmana Basu, who would be shortly described as progenitors of non-brahmana and brahmana priests respectively in the same account,[3] would be able to lift it. When finally Savara Jara and brahmana Basu were engaged to lift the *daru* "the Savara could lift easily while the brahmana with difficulty as at the command of Sri Krsna it suggested who is higher and who is lower or junior" (in status or hierarchy).[4] This episode has not been mentioned in the earlier versions of the tradition. Therefore, the motivation behind the creation and incorporation of this episode in the traditional account was to raise the status and position of the Daitas, the supposed descendants of the Savara Jara in which the log lifting capability has been devised as the measuring rod to determine who is superior between the two classes of priests: the brahmanas and the non-brahmanas (i.e. the Daitas).

Finally the same *Sarala Mahabharata* version of the tradition otherwise also sought to establish the superiority of the Daitas in another episode. There it is depicted that Nila Madhava cursed the king Galaba that his line or *vamsa* would be extinct as he (Galaba) had killed the Savaras, his (i.e., Nila Madhava's) sons.[5] In that connection Nila Madhava narrated how he himself had married a Savara girl in the *satyayuga* and in consequence earned the epithet or title Savari Narayana for himself.[6] This has also not been found mentioned in the earlier versions of the tradition. Equating the Savaras with the sons of Nila Madhava, the earlier incarnation of Lord Jagannatha, and threatening with a dire punishment when the Savaras are harmed and finally establishing matrimonial relationship between Visnu *alias* Nila

Madhava *alias* Lord Jagannatha and a Savara girl the restructured tradition-cum-origin myth quite clearly sought to safeguard and elevate the position of the Daitas, the descendants or progeny of the Savara chief Jara, in the cult hierarchy as well as in the Hindu society. It is quite significant in this connection that the Savaras (or Sauras or Soras), the supposed ancestors of the Daitas, have been depicted as the sons of Nila Madhava because the Daitas are treated as the kins of Lord Jagannatha in the cult of Jagannatha. As such they perform the funeral rites and observe the period of impurity caused by the death of a kin as per the scriptural instructions during the *Navakalevara* or periodic renewal of the images as has been mentioned in detail earlier.[7] It may be pointed out here that Sarala Das, popularly known as Sudramuni, being a non-brahmana himself had his natural sympathy for the Daitas, the non-brahmana priests. It is also significant in this connection that his *Mahabharata* was derided by the brahmanas of his time.[8]

Another such restructured tradition is to be found recorded in the *Rajabhoga* section of *Madala Panji*, the chronicle of the Jagannatha temple, Puri. The earlier version of this tradition is to be found in *Ramanuja Divya Caritai* and *Prapannamrta*. The later work is ascribed to Anantacarya. According to the *Rajabhoga* version of the tradition one Acarya (both *Ramanuja Divya Caritai* and *Prapannamrta* identify this Acarya with Acarya Ramanuja, but *Rajabhoga* does not mention the name and places the incident during the reign of Purushottama Deva of Solar dynasty who is separated from Ramanuja by more than three hundred years) was sorry to observe that the temple servants (*sevaka*), i.e., the priests of Jagannatha were neither observing the rules of purity nor performing the rituals as per the scriptural prescription. He made complains to the king against the priests. The king ordered the priests to observe the rules of purity and perform the rituals properly as per the wishes of the Goswami or Acarya. The priests in turn protested against this interference to Jagannatha, the Great Lord. That night the

Acarya was commanded (by Lord Jagannatha) not to interfere in the affairs of the temple servants (*sevaka*) or priests of the *ksetra* (i.e., Puri). He was asked to go to *Kurma Ksetra* (= Sri Kurmam) situated in the present state of Andhra Pradesh. According to *Rajabhoga* but not others, the same night the king was told (in a dream) that these priests had been close associates of the Lord during the Lord's incarnation as Krsna as cowherds and they never observed any rule of purity then. Therefore, they could not be forsaken/abandoned simply because of that reason and their services cannot be spared.[9]

It seems that in this *Rajabhoga* tradition only a section of the priests, in other words only the non-brahmana priests or the Daitas, have been meant by the term *sevaka* (i.e., temple servant) as they were supposed to be ignorant of the rules of purity and not adept in Brahmanic rituals, being non-brahmanas. It must be mentioned here that the earlier version of this tradition, as found in *Ramanuja Divya Caritai* and *Prapannamrta*, might not have been created in its entirety by the non-brahmana priests and might have some historical basis.[10] In this earlier version the temple servants (*sevaka*), i.e., the non-brahmana priests or the Daitas have not been described as the close associates of Krsna-Jagannatha in the *dvapara* age (*yuga*) which is found only in the *Rajabhoga* version of the tradition. Therefore, it may be concluded that the earlier tradition was sought to be restructured and converted into their origin myth by the Daitas and as a result at least only this part of the tradition (i.e., the Daitas were the close associates of Krsna-Jagannatha in the *dvapara* age) was added to the earlier tradition. Not only was this 'discovery' made but also this declaration was made by no less an authority than Lord Jagannatha himself. That made the claim sound much more authentic. Equally significant is the fact that the *bhakti* or devotion has been assigned a higher place than the *karma* or Brahmanic ritual in this tradition as the non-brahmana priests, i.e., the Daitas were not at all adept in the rituals. It may be further concluded that the Daitas thought it necessary to transform an earlier tradition and restructure, modify and convert it into their origin myth as they themselves felt threatened and perhaps realized that their origin was under clouds of suspicion or even challenged.

It should also be pointed out here that the *Rajabhoga* section of the *Madala Panji* is mainly a collection of priestly tradition collected (and perhaps selected) and then compiled and recorded by the temple servants if not by the real priests among the temple servants. Therefore it mainly recorded the traditions representing the points of view of the temple servants and especially priests who are their leaders. Of course as a set of copies of the different sections of *Madala Panji* used to be kept in the palace of the kings, the temple servants in charge of recording the *Rajabhoga* section of *Madala Panji* must have seen to it that the feelings of the contemporary kings were never hurt. But this is not relevant here. What is relevant is the fact that the Karanas who were in charge of the compilation and recording of the different sections of *Madala Panji* were themselves non-brahmanas. Therefore, it is quite likely that they had their sympathy for the non-brahmana priests, i.e., the Daitas.

On the whole a series of restructured and modified tradition-cum-origin myths show that the Daitas were perhaps apprehensive and worried for their own survival as priests of Lord Jagannatha and on the defensive as well as also aspired for upward mobility and elevation of their position in the cult and Hindu society. With that intention they restructured and modified some of the earlier traditions, which they expected would help them in their endeavour and facilitate their upward mobility or even their final absorption into the Hindu society.

Now the question arises why and in what circumstances a section of the Daitas claimed a separate identity for themselves as Sudha Suaras between the fifteenth century, the date of *Sarala Mahabharata* and the late sixteenth/early seventeenth century, the probable date of the *Karmangi* or the late seventeenth/early eighteenth century, the probable date of *Deula Tola* by (Sisu) Krsna Das a span of one hundred fifty to three hundred years.

It appears that the effort of the Daitas to elevate their position and get completely absorbed in the Hindu society succeeded, but only in a limited way. The *Sarala Mahabharata* version of the Nila Madhava-Jagannatha tradition and the *Rajabhoga* version of the earlier Ramanuja tradition could not facilitate their final absorption into the higher strata of Hindu society. If at all it placed them at the lowest rung of the *jati*-ladder and reminding them as well as everybody else of their Savara origin equated them with the untouchables in the Hindu society. It is indeed ironical that instead of helping them to elevate their position these restructured tradition-cum-origin myths became instrumental to downgrade them. It seems this situation rather compelled a section of ambitious Daitas to participate in the *jati*-mobility assuming a new name and claiming a separate identity for themselves.

The new name they assumed is, interestingly enough, Sudha Suara, because perhaps the Daitas were originally a sub-class/sub-branch of the Sudha class/branch of the Savara hill tribe as has been discussed earlier. It seems the original name 'Sudha' was not completely forgotten by this time though the name Saura had become Suara as per the rule of sound change called metathesis.[11] And the homophonous nature of this changed pronunciation Suara with the name of another group of temple servants, the Suaras (derived from the Sanskrit word *supakara*) or cooks provided them with an opportunity to raise their position in the hierarchy of the temple servants equating the Sudha Suaras, a sub-category of the Daitas with the Suaras, the cooks. At the least the homophonous nature of these two terms created an ambiguity from which they were likely only to gain in their effort to get absorbed in a higher strata of the Hindu society. These were perhaps the reasons for which they assumed this new name, Sudha Suara, for themselves. As a result they were not only accepted to be the holy or purified temple-cooks but as such they were assumed to be brahmanas as Jakob Rosel does.[12] It may be remembered here that for similar reasons the Sudhas, other than the priestly Sudhas, residing in the district of Puri also tried to move up the *jati*-ladder for which they tried to identify themselves either with the Khandayats or ksatriyas or even Casas (Cultivators) of the district of Puri.

After assuming this new name, Sudha Suara, for themselves their next logical step, in their effort for upward mobility in the *jati*-ladder, was to further restructure and remodify the already restructured and modified Nila Madhava-Jagannatha tradition as found in the *Sarala Mahabharata* and transform it into another origin myth or in other words a dual origin myth which not only traced the origin of the Daitas but also the origin of the Sudha Suaras. This further restructured and remodified tradition is to be found recorded in *Deula Tola* by (Sisu) Krsna Das.

The most important aspect of this further restructuring and remodification was to create a new and very interesting female character named 'Lalita'. In a way this character was not completely new as in the earlier modified or transformed version of the tradition as found in the *Sarala Mahabharata* the name Lalita is also mentioned. But there is an important difference. According to this earlier modified *Sarala Mahabharata* version of the tradition the name of the original Savara worshipper of Nila Madhava is Jara *alias* Basu and the name of his wife is Lalita.[13] Further, according to this version of the tradition, the brahmana who came in search of Nila Madhava is also named Basu. When the brahmana Basu arrived in the Savara hamlet in search of Nila Madhava he was well received by the Savara Jara *alias* Basu who, their names being identical (Basu in both the cases), established ritual kinship or brotherhood with the brahmana.[14] But at the same time the Savara was suspicious and reluctant to take the brahmana, his ritual kin, into confidence, share his secrets with him and show him Nila Madhava and the secret place of worship. But when Lalita, his (Savara's) wife, took fancy to the brahmana, her husband's ritual brother or *mitra*, and put pressure on her husband then only the reluctant Savara agreed to share the secret and later showed the brahmana both the secretly worshipped deity Nila Madhava and the secret place of worship.[15]

But in the further restructured and remodified tradition, as found in *Deula Tola* the original tribal worshipper of Nila Madhava is named Basu and his daughter (*and not wife*) is named Lalita. The name of the brahmana who came in search of Visnu or Nila Madhava is Bidyapati (and not Basu) according to this further restructured and remodified tradition. In fact, there was no necessity to give them (the Savara and the brahmana) identical names, which normally facilitates the ritual kinship or brotherhood, as will be explained a little later. After the arrival of the brahmana, Lalita, the Savara girl, fell in love with him. Learning this, her father compelled the brahmana to marry his daughter and threatened to kill him if he did not. In course of their conversation the brahmana suspected that the Savara was associated with Nila Madhava and knew where the deity was to be found. Then he married the Savara girl. After the marriage Lalita not only shared the secret with her husband but also put pressure on her father to show her husband the secret place of worship. Her father though reluctantly agreed to show his son-in-law the deity on her earnest appeal but was not prepared to show him the path leading to the secret place of worship. Therefore, he took the brahmana, his son-in-law, blindfolded to the place of worship. But with the active connivance nay conspiracy of his Savara wife the brahmana could discover the path leading to the secret place of worship. So, there is a great difference between the Lalita character of the earlier restructured and modified tradition as found in *Sarala Mahabharata* and the further restructured and remodified tradition found in *Deula*

Tola. Therefore, one may claim that it was a completely new character introduced for the first time in *Deula Tola*.

As it appears this further restructured and remodified version of the tradition is really more natural and much more romantic. It is somewhat unnatural to be more sympathetic towards the ritual brother/kin of one's husband and share the secrets of one's husband with him as has been shown in the *Sarala Mahabharata* version of the tradition. On the other hand it is much more natural and likely to be more attached to one's own husband than one's father and share one's father's secrets with one's own husband, or even actually take part in a conspiracy with one's husband against the father as the *Deula Tola* version of the tradition shows. Further with the addition of this love element between the Savara maiden and the brahmana young man the story has become more romantic and more attractive. Again their joint conspiracy against their father/father-in-law converted the tradition almost into a thriller. All these made this further restructured and remodified version of the tradition much more popular and now the common people of Orissa only know this further restructured and remodified version of the tradition, which has almost completely replaced the other versions of the tradition. This was only made possible by the creation of this character, Lalita.

But that was not the only aim, or even the primary aim of further restructuring and remodifying the tradition, and creating the Lalita character. The primary aim, as has been hinted earlier, was to convert this tradition into a dual origin myth and facilitate the upward mobility of the Sudha Suaras in the *jati*-ladder. It must be mentioned here that according to the earlier restructured and modified *Sarala Mahabharata* version of the tradition the brahmana Basu (Bidyapati of *Deula Tola*) who came in search of Nila Madhava had a brahmana wife and their off-spring/ descendants became brahmana priests and the descendants of the original Savara worshipper (Jara *alias* Basu) became the

Daitas or non-brahmana priests of Purusottama-Jagannatha as has been pointed out earlier. But with the primary purpose of legitimizing the emergence of the Sudha Suaras, a sub-category of the Daitas, and facilitating their upward mobility in *jati*-ladder, the character of Lalita, the daughter of the original Savara worshipper, was created. She was made to marry the brahmana, who came in search of Nila Madhava, so that the Sudha Suaras could get the opportunity to claim that they were the descendants or the off-springs of the union between the brahmana male and the Savara female. As a result not only they in turn could claim a separate identity for themselves different from the Daitas but at the same time could also claim brahmana blood in their vein without completely disowning and discarding their tribal or Savara origin (which would have been perhaps very difficult at this stage, if not impossible). In other words they could claim themselves to be half-brahmanas or semi-brahmanas which could help them in their upward mobility while at the same time indirectly taking credit for the discovery of Nila Madhava leading ultimately to the emergence of the cult of Jagannatha as the descendants of the Savara girl Lalita. As the Sudha Suaras were a sort of priests in the temple of Jagannatha they had no other go but to adopt the Brahmanic model in the *jati* mobility. For this reason Lalita was made to marry the brahmana. Had they adopted the ksatriya model of *jati* mobility, it is quite likely that Lalita would have been made to marry the king (Indradyumna or Gala). Not only that in the patriarchal Hindu society the caste of the father mostly prevails and counts in the case of *anuloma* type of inter-caste marriages of the parents, i.e., "when a male of higher *varna* marries a woman of a lower *varna*",[16] which assured them (the Sudha Suaras) full brahmanahood ultimately. But while the Sudha Suaras were adopting the Brahmanic model because of their priestly profession and status at the shrine of Lord Jagannatha the other Sudhas residing in the District of Puri were adopting ksatriya model in their upward mobility in the *jati*-ladder as has already been pointed out earlier. On the whole the creation of the Lalita character in this further restructured and remodified tradition immensely facilitated the upward mobility of the Sudha Suaras, a section of the Daitas, in the *jati*-ladder. Therefore, one tends to conclude that in *Deula Tola* the Lalita character was conceived and created with a definite purpose behind it which was to provide a section of Daitas an opportunity to successfully participate in the *jati* mobility in their effort to get absorbed into the Hindu society.

Geib perhaps thinks that the primary purpose behind the creation or rather the transformation of the Lalita character in *Deula Tola* was to legitimize the (Sudha) Suaras, a 'Mischklasse', the off-spring of mixed marriages between the *Pujapandas* (i.e., the brahmana priests) on one hand and the Daitas on the other, providing the Sudha Suaras with mythical parents and Brahmanic or at least semi-Brahmanic pedigree. He (Geib) gives a broad hint to that effect.[17] Geib almost believes what the author of the *Deula Tola* text wanted people to believe. As the mixed marriage between the brahmana, supposed to be the progenitor of the brahmana priests, i.e., the *Pujapandas*, and the Savara maiden has been mentioned in *Deula Tola*, Geib comes to the conclusion that mixed marriages between the brahmana *Pujapandas* on one hand and the non-brahmana Daitas, supposed to be of Savara origin, on the other, had indeed taken place and the Sudha Suaras, as the *Deula Tola* text suggests, are off-springs of such mixed marriages. Further he also believes that the Sudha Suaras, the off-spring of such mixed marriages, were in need of some kind of legitimation which, to some extent, was provided to them by a set of mythical parents, the brahmana male Bidyapati and the Savara female Lalita in the *Deula Tola* text.

This rather betrays Geib's tendency to seek to discover the historical basis, if any, of the traditional account instead of studying the historical background and circumstances leading to its emergence and evolution. In the present work, as has been explained earlier, the former, conventional method of analysing the traditional account has been rejected and a radically different method adopted which seeks to study the background and circumstances of its emergence at the first place and, later its evolution through modification, if any.

Moreover the conventional method of analysis provides too simplistic an explanation and cannot be accepted. Further the creation of such a character and making her marry the brahmana Bidyapati, supposed to be the ancestor of the *Pujapandas*, instead of legitimizing the inter-caste marriage between the Daitas and the *Pujapandas*, would have only prevented it as the marriage between the descendants of father's kins and mother's kins is prohibited by the local custom. Geib has also not been able to explain why they assumed the name Sudha Suara in that case, i.e., if they were the off-spring of mixed marriages. Rather the truth seems to be the other way round. In other words the Sudha Suaras are not the outcome of mixed marriage as Geib believes though this was claimed in order to facilitate the upward mobility of the Sudha Suaras in the *jati*-ladder. Had the Sudha Suaras really been the off-spring of mixed marriage they would never have been in need of such legitimation, which as Geib believes, was provided to them through an imagined mixed marriage and a set of mythical parents. Instead — as the Sudha Suaras were simply not the off-spring of mixed marriage and mixed parentage — the mixed marriage between a brahmana male and a Savara female was imagined and a set of mythical parents were provided to them by the *Deula Tola* text so that they could 'falsely' claim their descent from a mixed marriage and mixed parentage. If at all they were in need of a different kind of legitimation and there is a subtle difference between these two kinds of legitimation.

Therefore the creation or really the transformation of the Lalita character in the *Deula Tola* text served the primary purpose of facilitating the absorption and upward mobility of the Sudha Suaras, a sub-branch of the Daita branch of the Sudhas, a sub-class of the Savara/Saura or Sora tribals, in the Hindu society but not legitimizing the off-spring of mixed marriages.

But this further restructuring and remodification had perhaps also another secondary purpose. This further remodification, in fact, established some kind of blood relationship between the two major categories of the temple priests, i.e., the brahmana priests (supposed to be the descendants of the brahmana who came in search of Nila Madhava) and the non-brahmana priests or the Daitas (supposed to be the descendants of the original Savara worshipper) introducing a third major category of the temple priests, the Sudha Suaras who could imagine and claim blood relationship with the brahmana priests on one hand and the non-brahmana priests or the Daitas on the other. In other words the brahmana priests being the descendants of the brahmana, who came in search of Nila Madhava, and his brahmana wife are related to the Sudha Suaras, who are the descendants of the same brahmana and his Savara wife, Lalita, the father being common to both the groups. Again as the Sudha Suaras are also related to the Daitas as the latter (i.e., the Daitas) are only the descendants of Lalita's father while the Sudha Suaras are the descendants of Lalita (and her brahmana husband). As the Sudha Suaras are related to both the brahmana priests and the non-brahmana priests (i.e., the Daitas) these two categories or groups of priests are also related to each other albeit indirectly. This established an emotional bond and some kind of unity among these three different major and also perhaps warring groups or categories of temple priests in their common fight against the interferences of the Rajas of Khurda in the affairs of the temple and the cult of Jagannatha, taking advantage of the disunity and infighting among them.

It is really interesting to note how a highly serious scholar like Geib has completely been taken in by such imagined and falsely claimed blood relationship between the brahmana priests on one hand and non-brahmana priests on the other indirectly through a third category of semi-brahmana/half-brahmana priests, the

Sudha Suaras. Though he did not explicitly mention it Geib's belief is reflected in his claim that the Sudha Suaras are a 'Mischklass', off-spring of mixed marriage between the *Pujapandas*, i.e., the brahmana priests and the Daitas, i.e., the non-brahmana priests. Therefore Geib, who believes in the indirect blood relationship between the two major and influential categories of temple priests, has not been able to grasp the real purpose behind such false claim of blood relationship which was to bring about some sort of emotional unity among the various categories of temple priests in their common struggle against the interference of the Rajas of Khurda in the administration of the temple of Jagannatha and perhaps also to present to the outside world the picture of a unified body of the temple priests. This also makes it amply clear how successful the attempt must have been to influence the people in general and the temple priests in particular in creating a false belief in their mind regarding the blood relationship existing among the various categories of temple priests through the *Deula Tola* text though in reality no such blood relationship ever existed. If a highly serious scholar like Geib could be led to believe in such a false claim of blood relationship it is small wonder that the common people and particularly the temple servants were easily taken in by such false claim and indeed believed in the same.

That the royal interference in the affairs of the cult of Jagannatha and in the administration of the temple was a reality and was opposed and resisted by the temple priests in the medieval period leading to such a false claim can be deduced by studying the possible motive(s) behind more than one episode incorporated in the *Sarala Mahabharata* version of the tradition. The previously mentioned log-lifting episode is one such episode. It has already been pointed out that this episode seeks to establish the superiority of the Daitas, i.e., the non-brahmana priests, represented by the Savara Jara, over the brahmana priests, represented by the brahmana Basu, as, according to this episode, when the holy log was lifted by Jara and Basu the Savara could lift it easily whereas the brahmana with difficulty. But not only that, this particular episode also seeks to establish the superiority of the priests in general (i.e., both the brahmana and the non-brahmana priests) over the kings of Orissa, represented by the king Indradyumna as he, engaging all the forces at his command, was not able to get the holy log lifted from the Rohini Kunda which could be finally done by the brahmana Basu and the Savara Jara.[18] This attempt to establish the superiority of the priests in general over the kings of Orissa reveals the concern of the priests at the royal interference in the affairs of the cult and their opposition to the same. Similarly Nila Madhava-Jagannatha cursing the king Gala that king Gala's line would be extinct as he had killed his (i.e., Nila Madhava-Jagannatha's) sons, the innocent Savaras, is another such episode incorporated also in the *Sarala Mahabharata* tradition which too indirectly reveals this royal interference in the affairs of the cult and the opposition to that by the non-brahmana priests.

The reflection of the royal interference in the affairs of the cult and the resultant priestly opposition to it in the episode of seeking a strange or unusual favour or boon by king Indradyumna from Lord Jagannatha in the further restructured and remodified version of the traditional account to be found in *Deula Tola*, and occurring almost at the very end of it, is even more explicit and more direct. As has already been pointed out in the *Sarala Mahabharata* version of the tradition Nila Madhava-Jagannatha *alias* Visnu cursed the king Gala or Galaba that his line (*vamsa*) would be extinct as he had killed the innocent Savaras, his (Nila Madhava-Jagannatha's) sons. In contrast the same motif occurs in the *Deula Tola* version in a greatly modified or sharply twisted form. In the *Deula Tola* version Lord Jagannatha does not curse the king with the extinction of his line. Instead the king Indradyumna, as opposed to the king Gala of *Sarala Mahabharata* version, seeks a very strange boon or unusual favour from the Lord that his line be extinct. Surprised the Lord wants to know the reason for this rather strange or peculiar request. Indradyumna then explains that he does not want to have a descendant lest a descendant of his, overcome with vanity, should claim to be the owner/custodian of the temple of Jagannatha, the headquarters of the cult. And in that case all the merit (*dharma* or *punya*) of construction will be lost or gone.[19] In other words, Indradyumna was afraid that one of his descendants might claim exclusive right over the temple and in the affairs of the cult. Pleased with this explanation the Lord then granted this favour to king Indradyumna.

This sharply twisted motif is found mentioned for the first time in a Bengali version of the tradition incorporated into *Caitanya Mangal*, a biographical work on Caitanya in verse form, written by Jayananda in the sixth decade of the sixteenth century.[20] But the incorporation of this motif in *Deula Tola*, a work of late seventeenth or early eighteenth century, is quite significant. It indicates that this motif continued to serve its purpose from the sixteenth through early eighteenth centuries. But what was the real purpose behind this motif? It appears that the purpose was to deny the kings of Orissa (and later the Rajas of Khurda having the *de jure* control over the temple of Jagannatha since the late sixteenth century) the exclusive right over the cult and deny their right to interfere in the affairs of the cult affair and the temple administration as such a royal interference could have been against the express wish of Indradyumna, the original founder king of the cult, who is supposed to have constructed the temple of Lord Jagannatha. Obviously the priests of the temple of Jagannatha had good reasons to be concerned at the royal interference in temple affairs. It is quite significant in this connection that this episode of seeking a very unusual favour or strange boon is found in all the versions of the *Deula Tola* group of texts[21] and the inclusion of this motif in all the versions of the *Deula Tola* group of texts only reveals that this was a common cause though there were differences and even rivalry and competition among the various sections or categories of the temple servants and even the temple priests.

Geib of course interprets this motif differently. In Orissa till recently the popular belief was that the existing temple of Jagannatha at Puri had been constructed by one Anangabhima Deva of the Ganga dynasty. This belief is reflected in a traditional verse,[22] in the *Rajabhoga* section of the *Madala Panji*,[23] in Odradesa/Kataka Rajavamsavali, a part of Mackenzie Collection, prepared in the early nineteenth century[24] and also in *Gangavamsanucaritam*, a *campu kavyam*, written some time in the eighteenth century.[25] When the history of Orissa was reconstructed for the first time in the nineteenth century the early historians like Stirling, Hunter, R.L. Mitra and Pyarimohan Acharya almost completely depended on the traditional accounts and especially on the *Rajabhoga* section of the *Madala Panji* as source of information. As a result they not only provided an erroneous genealogy of the Ganga kings of Orissa but gave the full credit for the construction of the temple of Jagannatha to the Anangabhima Dev of that genealogy.[26] In the last decade of the last century M.M. Chakravarti discovered two sets of copper-plate inscriptions of Narasimha IV of the Gaṅga dynasty containing the subsequently famous Gaṅga *prasasti* (eulogy) and on the basis of that for the first time furnished the correct and almost the complete genealogy of the Gaṅga kings of Orissa.[27] On the basis of a *sloka* or stanza in the same *prasasti* he also came to the conclusion that the existing temple of Jagannatha at Puri was built by Chodaganga Deva, the founder of the Gaṅga dynasty of Orissa and not by Anangabhima though he gets the credit in the tradition.[28] Even after that some scholars like Krupasindhu Mishra, Jagabandhu Singh and P. Mukherjee who were not at all prepared to reject the tradition altogether tried to present a compromise formula regarding the construction of the temple of Jagannatha: that Chodaganga commenced the construction of the temple which was completed during the reign of either Anangabhima II or Anangabhima III of the Gaṅga dynasty.[29] But subsequently after the discovery of the Dasagoba copper-plate inscription of Rajaraja III, the son of Anangabhima II and father of Anangabhima III,[30] wherein the same stanza giving full credit for the construction of the temple to Chodaganga occurs for the first time which has been repeated in all the later copper-plate inscriptions of the Gaṅga kings including the Nagari plates of Anangabhima III and the earlier mentioned plates of Narasimha IV, discovered by Chakravarti, most of the scholars gradually have come round to the opinion that the temple was really constructed by Chodaganga though the credit for the same was given to Anangabhima in the tradition because of a confusion.[31]

According to Geib this motif of seeking the most unusual favour by Indradyumna from Lord Jagannatha can be interpreted as an indirect but critical reference to this state of affairs, i.e., the construction of the temple by Chodaganga but the credit going to Anangabhima, one of Chodaganga's descendants.[32] But this again betrays Geib's tendency to discover a historical basis — if any — of the traditional account or at least of a single element or motif of the traditional account. Instead, an attempt should be made to discover the real purpose hidden behind such elements or motifs and whose — if an individual's or group's — interest or cause they really served in the past and also perhaps serve in the present. Further Geib's proposition is not only far-fetched but also highly improbable because for centuries the people believed that the temple of Jagannatha was constructed either by the mythical king Indradyumna or by the historical king Anangabhima and did not even suspect that the credit for the construction of the temple was being given to the wrong person, i.e., to one of the descendants of Chodaganga, whereas he himself really constructed it. When the people including the authors of the *Deula Tola* group of texts did not even know that the temple was in fact constructed, not by one of his descendants, but by Chodaganga himself, the question of the credit given to the wrong person in the minds of the people, especially in the minds of the authors of the *Deula Tola* group of texts, does not arise at all. In that case the further question of its indirect and perhaps critical reference and reflection in the *Deula Tola* group of texts or

Caitanya Mangal cannot even be imagined. Further the issue of the construction of the existing temple of Jagannatha at Puri is not yet finally settled. H. von Stietencron has recently advanced weighty arguments to the effect that the temple was really completed during the reign of Anangabhima III, supporting the popular tradition.[33] Therefore, Geib's interpretation is unacceptable and the seeking of the most unusual favour by Indradyumna cannot be linked to that.

Besides in two of the *Deula Tola* group of texts written by Dama Das and Magunia Das the concerns and anxieties of the temple servants (i.e., *sevakas*) over the interference of the kings of Khurda in the affairs of the cult of Jagannatha and in the administration of the temple have been reflected in the seeking of another strange favour on the part of king Indradyumna which has not been mentioned in other versions, including the *Sarala Mahabharata* version, of the tradition. According to these two *Deula Tola* texts, Indradyumna as a favour also wanted that nobody should ever find any fault with the *sevakas*, i.e., the temple servants.[34] This is just to prevent the kings of Khurda from finding fault with the temple servants including the priests even in case of gross dereliction of duties and indiscipline. In other words this favour sought to deny the kings of Khurda even the *de jure* control over the administration of the temple.

On the basis of what has so far been said it may be concluded that from fifteenth century, i.e., the date of *Sarala Mahabharata*, and especially from the sixteenth century, i.e., the date of *Caitanya Mangal* by Jayananda, through eighteenth century, i.e., the date of *Deula Tola*, the temple servants (*sevakas*) in general and the priests in particular of the temple of Jagannatha at Puri were very much concerned about interferences of the kings of Orissa and subsequently of the Rajas of Khurda, who succeeded them, in the affairs of the cult of Jagannatha and in the general administration of the temple. Some other circumstantial evidences also corroborate this conclusion.[35] Therefore, it is quite natural that all the concern and anxiety over the interferences of the kings got reflected in *Sarala Mahabharata*, *Caitanya Mangal* and *Deula Tola* especially in the *Deula Tola* in the episode of king Indradyumna seeking a strange favour that his line (vamsa) be extinct — from Lord Jagannatha which indirectly denied the kings of Khurda any moral right whatsoever in the affairs of the cult and temple administration.

The only logical extension of the concern and anxiety is to try to bring about a unity and forge a common or united front of the various categories or sections of temple servants and especially of the priests, who were only the natural leaders of all types of temple servants, in order to resist and successfully prevent such royal interference in the affairs of the cult and temple administration. And, as has been mentioned earlier, the creation of the character Lalita, the Savara girl, took a positive step in that direction.

The attempt of the Sudha Suaras, a sub-category of the Daitas, for upward mobility in the *jati*-ladder, through a process of further restructuring and remodification of the traditional account, could have been opposed and resisted by both the brahmana priests and the non-brahmana priests, i.e., the Daitas which was quite natural but for the dire necessity of forging a common or united front against their common source of danger, the Rajas of Khurda, for the protection of their own rights, interests, privileges, pecuniary benefits and influential position in the cult affairs and the temple administration. The further restructured and remodified version of the traditional account, the result of the process of upward mobility on the part of the Sudha Suaras, provided the brahmana priests as well as the Daitas an opportunity to bring about a unity among the various categories and sub-categories of the priests though at the same time undermining and successfully neutralizing their natural tendency to oppose and resist such upward mobility. Therefore the normally expected opposition and resistance to the upward mobility of the Sudha Suaras could not materialize. Again, as the Sudha Suaras adopted the brahmana model for their upward mobility in the *jati*-ladder normally the resistance of the brahmana priests would have been more vehement in this case. But the brahmana priests preferred to ignore and close their eyes to the attempt at such upward mobility on the part of the Sudha Suaras as now they could quite naturally secure for themselves the leadership of a unified body of various categories of priests in their common struggle against the Rajas of Khurda, which such upward mobility provided. Perhaps they themselves were more keen to form a common front against the Rajas of Khurda as they were the chief beneficiary and expected to benefit most out of it.

Therefore the creation or transformation of the character Lalita, the Savara girl in the further restructured and remodified version of the Nila Madhava-Jagannatha tradition, as found in *Deula Tola* by (Sisu) Krsna Das served several different purposes. Besides the primary purpose of facilitating the upward mobility of a section of Daitas or the non-brahmana priests, the Sudha Suaras, in the *jati*-ladder it served the secondary, nevertheless important, purpose of forging a unity among the various sections of the temple priests against the royal interference in the cult affairs and temple administration. Further giving the story a realistic as well as romantic touch at the same time it elevated the literary value of the work and also ensured its success as a literary piece and its popularity.

Besides these major differences, i.e., the creation of the character Lalita, the Savara girl, and introducing the episode of seeking a very strange or unusual favour by king Indradyumna that his line be extinct, there are also other minor differences between the primary restructured and modified *Sarala Mahabharata* version and the further restructured and re-modified *Deula Tola* version of the Nila Madhava-Jagannatha tradition with the similar objective. As for example in this further restructured and remodified version the tribal or the Savara worshipper retains the name Basu (from Visva Vasu of *Skanda Purana* version) but the brahmana who comes in search of Nila Madhava and later marries the Savara girl, Lalita is called Bidyapati (from Vidyapati of the *Skanda Purana* version) instead of Basu, as *Sarala Mahabharata* calls him. In other words the *Deula Tola* version follows the Sanskrit *Skanda Purana* version instead of Oriya *Sarala Mahabharata* version as far as the names of the original Savara worshipper and the brahmana explorer are concerned. The reason is simple. The Savara and the brahmana did not any more require to have identical names because there was no necessity to forge or establish ritual kinship between them, leading to the discovery of Nila Madhava and the secret place of worship by the brahmana, as in the *Deula Tola* version the brahmana was to marry the daughter of the Savara by which act they were made kins by marriage. Moreover by following the *Skanda Purana* version not only the *Deula Tola* version appeared to be much more authentic than the *Sarala Mahabharata* version but the name Bidyapati could also serve several different purposes: (1) firstly linking the Patis or Pati Mahapatras, a section of brahmana priests, the brahmana counterpart of the Daitas, with Bidyapati because of the partial similarity between the two names it indirectly hinted that Pati or Pati Mahapatras are the descendants of mythical Bidyapati especially because brahmanas with Pati surnames or family names are found in Orissa; (2) secondly because of this linkage between Bidyapati and the Pati priests the tradition appeared to be even more authentic; and (3) thirdly this act of linking not only elevated the status of the Patis as descendants of mythical Bidyapati but also indirectly elevated the status of the Daitas, as the non-brahmana counterpart of the Patis, facilitating their absorption into the Hindu society.

From the above discussion it is now clear how the Sudha Suaras, a section/branch of the Daitas, further restructured and remodified the Nila Madhava-Jagannatha tradition and converted it into their origin myth, to be found in the *Deula Tola* text by (Sisu) Krsna Das, with the primary aim of facilitating their upward mobility in the *jati*-ladder though it also served some secondary purposes. This is just an example of how a traditional account can play an active role in the *jati* mobility getting further restructured and remodified in the process.

Notes

1. When Ramanuja, the famous South Indian Vaisnava saint of *Visistadvaitavadin* school, visited Orissa and Puri — if at all — towards the end of the eleventh century the Puri deity/ deities was/were sufficiently Hinduized to have been able to attract his attention. For more information and a detailed discussion on his visit ***see*** Dash, G.N., 1978a: 157-61. By the fourteenth century Purusottama-Jagannatha of Puri was so famous and was considered so important as a Hindu deity that Sayana (*circa* 1300-1380), the famous commentator on the *Vedas*, linked this deity with a *mantra* (10th *Mandala*, 155 *Sukta*, 3rd *Mantra*) of *Ṛgveda*. **See** Padhi, B.M., 1975: 27-28 and Geib, 1975: 132, fn. 448.
2. Geib, 1975: 131, 180.
3. *Sarala Mahabharata, Musali Parba*, 12/151-53; ***see*** chap. 5, notes no. 15 and 16.
4. *brāhmaṇa āḍe taḍai śabara āḍe uṭhai/*
   srīkr̥ṣṇa ajnāre se ūca kaniṣṭhai//
   — *Sarala Mahabharata, Musali Parba*, 12/106
5. *mādhaba boiḷe rājā tu manda kr̥tya kalu/*
   sabara putranta mora kimpāī māilu// (9/63)
   ... ...
   mama bhagatanku kalu je jhingāsa/
   āho gālaba rājā tora na rahiba baṃśa// (9/83)
   — *Sarala Mahabharata, Musali Parba*
6. *Ibid.*, 9/70-71.

7. **See** chap. 5, note no. 10.
8. Manasinha, M. 1962: 53-54, 62-63 and Panigrahi, K.C., 1975: 17-18, 23.
9. *Madala Panji*, 1940: 49-50.
10. **See** Dash, G.N., 1978a: 157-61 for a more detailed discussion on this tradition.
11. **See** chap. 5, note no. 37 for the definition of the term metathesis.
12. Rosel, J., 1980: 54.
13. *laḷitā nāme sabaruṇī tāhāra gharaṇī/*
    dui jaṇahuṁ āna kehi tāhā na jāṇi //
    — *Sarala Mahabharata, Bana Parba*, 6/126

14.(a) *jārā śabara nāma hoye basu śabara boli/*
basu nāme brāhmaṇa bheṭila tāra palli//

. . . . . .

brāhmaṇa boilā mora nāma basudeba/
kirāta boilā bipra mora maitra hoiba//
— *Sarala Mahabharata, Musali Parba*, 8/20 and 25

(b) *jārā nāme kirāta je basu nāme dvija/*
beni nāma yekata maitra aiśurjya//
— *Sarala Mahabharata, Bana Parba*, 6/144

For more information on ritual kinship ***see*** Bhowmick, P.K., 1961: 116 and Mahapatra, L.K., 1973: 93-94.

15. *Sarala Mahabharata, Bana Parba*, Section 6.
16. For more information on the *anuloma* type of marriage, ***see*** Kane, P.V., 1941: 52. Of course Hindu *smṛti* writers are not unanimous that the caste of the father will determine the caste of the off-spring in case of *anuloma* type of marriage. **See** Kane, 1941: 55-58. But the local custom must be given the due weightage which ultimately prevails. It may be of interest in this connection that while discussing the institution of concubinage in Orissa O'Malley observed way back in 1932, "It is subject to the provision that the concubines must belong to clean castes. It has actually given rise to a distinct caste, the

Shagird peshas (meaning servants), which is some 50,000 strong. It consists of the off-springs of such irregular union and their descendants, and the fissiparous tendency of caste is shown by its being divided, according to the caste of the father (Brahman, Khandayat, Karan etc.), into separate sub-castes, between which there is no intermarriage." O'Malley, 1974: 95. It clearly points out how ultimately the caste of the father may prevail in case of the *anuloma* type of marriages.

17. Geib, 1975: 165, fn. no. 530; 170; 144, fn. no. 478.

18. *Sarala Mahabharata, Musali Parba*, 6/98-107.

19.(a) *tumbhe jebe bara deba maguachi muhĩ/*
mohara baṃśare prabhu na rahibe kehi//

. . . . . .

putra nāti bolibe je deuḷa mohara/
ambhara boile dharma nāśa jiba mora//

— *Deula Tola* by (Sisu) Krsna Das, Kohinoor Press edition, 1953: 20.

(b) *tumbhe jebe bara deba maguachi muhĩ/*
mohara baṃśare kehi na thibe gosāĩ//

. . . .

putra nāti bolibe je deuḷa āmbhara/
āmbhara boile dharma jiba je mohara//

— *Deula Tola* by (Sisu) Krsna Das, Dasarathi Pustakalaya edition, 1950: 26.

(c) *tume jebe bara deba māguachi muhĩ/*
mohara baṃśare na rahile kehi//

. . . .

putra nāti kahibe je deuḷa āmbhara/
āmbhara boile sabu dharma jiba mora//

— *Deula Tola* by (Sisu) Krsna Das, Prabhati Pustakalaya edition: 20-21.

20. *Caitanya Mangal, Prakash* 4/24-31 and *Prakash* 1/146.

21. As for example in *Deula Tola* texts by Magunia Das and Dama Das (and both Kanthi and ORP Manuscript versions of the text by Dama Das) the same very unusual favour has also been sought by Indradyumna.

(a) *māguchi bara ete muhī̃/*
mo baṃśe na rahibe kehi// (5/71)

. . . .

putra putrādi thile mora/
bolibe deuḷa āmbhara// (5/75)
je dharma karāiṇa thiba/
āmbha boile nāśa jiba// (5/76)
je dharma āpaṇe kariba/
pare ke dehe na kahiba// (5/77) : folio, 88b.

— *Deula Tola* by Magunia Das, K.C. Sahu, MSS.

(b) *dayā jadi kala mote prabhu bhābagrāhī/*
mohara baṃśare āu na rahibe kehi//
mohara deuḷa boli juge juge thiba/
āu kehi e deuḷa dābi na kariba//

— *Srīkṣetra Māhātmya bā Deula Tolā* by Damu Das, Kanthi edition, 1323: 58.

Of course this version of the text gives a completely different reason for the seeking of this unusual favour by Indradyumna. According to this version Indradyumna says that the temple should be known as his temple in ages to come and nobody should be able to claim the temple. Even this reason also supports the argument of the present work.

(c) *āhuri bareka deba māguachi muhī̃/*
mohara baṃśare prabhu na rahibe kehi//

. . . .

putra nāti bolibe je deuḷa āmbhara/
mohara boile dharma nāśa jiba mora//

— *Daru Brahma* by Dama Das, ORP Manuscript,

Paper Copy: 673. **See** above chap. 4, note no. 7 for more information on this text.

22. *śakāvde randhra śubhrāmsu rūpa nakṣatra nāyake/*

prāsada kārayāmāsananga bhīmena dhīmatā//

See Mukherjee, P., 1940: 31 and Stietencron, 1977: 525 and also 531, fn. no. 47.

23. *Madala Panji*, 1940: 27-34.

24. *Odradesa Rajavamsavali*, 1983:16.

Kataka Rajavamsavali, 1987: 20. Both *Odradesa Rajavamsavali* and *Kataka Rajavamsavali* are in fact two different versions of the same text. **See** *Kataka Rajavamsavali*, Introduction: 5.

25. *Gangavamsanucarita*, 1979: 175.

26.(a) For Andrew Stirling ***see*** Sahu, N.K. (ed.), 1956b: 236.

(b) For W.W. Hunter ***see*** Sahu, N.K. (ed.), 1956a: 200.

(c) Mitra, R.L., Vol. 2, 1963: 183-84.

(d) Acharya, Pyarimohan, 1925: 73.

27. Chakravarti, M.M., 1895. The only name that did not figure in the genealogy of Ganga kings worked out by Chakravarti is Bhanudeva IV, the last Ganga king.

28.(a) *Ibid.* : 135. The stanza (*sloka*) concerned is the stanza No. 27 of the *prasasti* part of the inscription. In this connection Chakravarti observed, "The inscription then differs from the Madala Panji which ascribes the erection of the temple to Ananga-bhima-deva, and which gives several specific details. Is this difference due to the fact that the main temple was built by Codaganga, but that the side temples, the walls, & c., and the thorough systematisation of the ceremonies and sebas were made in the time of Ananga-bhima-deva, and that in course of time, the former circumstances was lost sight of and the temple passed as Ananga-bhima's?"

(b) Chakravarti, M.M., 1898a.

29.(a) Mishra, Krupasindhu, 1926: 103-04.

(b) Singh, J., 1964: 361.

(c) Mukherjee, P., 1940: 29-31.

30. Dasagoba copper-plate inscription has been edited by D.C. Sircar and S. Ratha Sarma in *Epigraphia Indica*, Vol. 31, 1955-56: 249-62.

31. The confusion supposedly arose out of the fact that Anangabhima III had constructed a temple for Purusottama (i.e. Jagannatha) at Cuttack as is known from his Nagari Copper-plate inscription. Nagari copper-plates have been edited by D.C. Sircar in *Epiagraphia Indica*, vol. 28. The construction of this temple at Cuttack got somehow mixed up in the minds of the people with the construction of the temple at Puri perhaps because of Anangabhima's patronage of the cult of Jagannatha and especially because of his declaration that the empire belongs to Lord Jagannatha and he was just merely his *rauta* (deputy/captain/viceroy) and his enthusiasm in various building activities. ***See*** Acharya, P., 1969b: 310-13.

32. Geib, 1975: 165, fn. no. 533.

33. Stietencron, H. von, 1977 and 1978b: 73-77.

34.(a) *e bara mote ājnā heba/*
sebaka dosa na dhariba// (5/65) : folio 88a
— *Deula Tola* by Magunia Das. K.C. Sahu MSS.

(b) *sebakanka dosa prabhu mane na dharibe/*
— *Daru Brahma* by Dama Das, ORP Manuscript Paper Copy: 671.

35. For some circumstantial evidences ***see*** Dash, G.N., 1976, 1978a and 1978b.

7
Conclusion

To sum up, in medieval period in Orissa, as well as in the other parts of India, aboriginal tribes were continuously getting Hinduized and absorbed into the Hindu society. Of the many channels of Hinduization like ksatriyaization open to them one was through the Hinduization of the tribal shrine or deity. The latter was also a part of the medieval state formation as in medieval period the Hinduization of the tribal shrine or deity was the result of the forces working simultaneously both from below, i.e., the Hinduization of the tribals through culture contact and also from above, i.e., the royal patronage and the Brahmanic acceptance of the tribal shrine/deity which was necessary for the consolidation of the royal power and the Brahmanic influence. This was especially true in the case of tribal shrine/deity having a strong association with a particular geographical territory inhabited by the tribals. This particular manner of Hinduization of the tribals through the Hinduization of the tribal shrine/deity as different from various other manners of Hinduization may be studied under a broad heading, '*ksetra*-centred-Hinduization' or an even broader heading, '*ksetra*-centred-Social Mobility'.

From among several different types of the *ksetra*-centred-Hinduization one type stands out insofar as it allows the original tribal priests of the tribal shrine/deity to continue to function as priests even after the Hinduization of the shrine/deity and to get Hinduized because of their association with the priestly profession.

This type of *ksetra*-centred-Hinduization may be termed 'Pujakaization' (from the Sanskrit word *pujaka* meaning worshipper and by extension priest) in the absence of a better term.

The Hinduization of the tribal shrine/deity, at the initial stage, resulted in the incorporation of some Brahmanic elements in the ritual of such tribal shrine/deity like the Brahmanic mode of worship and as a natural consequence the appointment of the brahmana priests. But at the same time the original tribal priests of the now Hinduized tribal shrine/deity were also allowed to continue and function as non-brahmana priests side by side with the newly appointed brahmana priests. These non-brahmana priests could not be completely dispended with and had to be retained, and their priestly rights, privileges and prerogatives had to be recognised and accepted as they formed a sort of cultural bridge between the tribal people inhabiting the area on one hand and the Hindu royalty and the brahmanas on the other. As both the political-military power or the royalty and the brahmanas needed the original tribal priests in order to strengthen their newly established bond with the now Hinduized tribal shrine/deity and through the same with the tribal population inhabiting the area as a part of the consolidation process of their own power and influence they (i.e., the original tribal priests) had to be retained.

Not only that. Precisely because of the same reason the newly created *ksetra mahatmya* or *sthala purana* type of traditional accounts — that invariably grows around any and every Hindu religious shrine/deity and which is an important feature of the ksetraization process, i.e., the process which facilitates a non-*ksetra* becoming a *ksetra*— which immediately started taking shape around the newly Hinduized tribal shrine/deity as a larger process of further Hinduization. Further in the same the close association of the autochthonous tribes with the pre-Hinduized phase of the now—Hinduized tribal shrine/deity, as the original worshipper, and their important role in the discovery and the origin of worship of the same had to be recognised and accepted — even in the Brahmanic version of the same tradition.

But in that connection one interesting point should be taken note of here. The fact that the tribals associated with the discovery and the origin of worship of the now—Hinduized tribal deity and the non-brahmana priests of the same are not only linked or connected but also they are one and the same was ignored and did not find any mention — may be deliberately — in the Brahmanic version of the *ksetra mahatmya* or *sthala purana* which was mostly in written form. This is not at all surprising as that would have only strengthened and enhanced the position and importance of the non-brahmana priests in the cult (perhaps again at the expense of the brahmana priests) who were after all the rivals and fellow competitors of the brahmana priests in the priestly profession. The brahmana priests who had a hand in the preparation of the Brahmanic version of the *ksetra mahatmya* or *sthala purana* never wanted that to happen. The priests of tribal origin had to be retained but their importance and influence had to be kept in check.

However the non-brahmana priests of the now Hinduized tribal shrine/deity and their descendants — functioning side by side with the brahmana priests — got an opportunity to get Hinduized. At the same time some kind of pressure was also brought to bear upon them to get Hinduized because they had to compete with the brahmana priests, their rivals in the priestly profession. Further after the initial phase of Hinduization of the tribal shrine/deity was over and after the royalty as well as the brahmanas consolidated their respective power and influence, at least to some extent, among the tribal population of the area — as meanwhile tribals were already Hinduized or were fast becoming Hinduized — they (i.e., the royalty and the brahmanas) were not in that much need of the non-brahmana priests to act as a cultural bridge. In addition to that the brahmana priests were also facing competition from the non-brahmana priests who were, in the public memory though not in the Brahmanic version of the *ksetra mahatmya* or *sthala purana* type of traditional account, associated with the discovery of the shrine/deity and the origin of the worship. Prompted by that reason they, quite naturally, wanted to minimize the role, importance and the position of the non-brahmana priests, if not to get rid of them completely at the now Hinduized shrine. That they were not brahmanas were not at all adept in the Brahmanic rituals; were not familiar with the Brahmanic rules of purity and were also not well conversant with the Brahmanic scriptures put them at a great disadvantage *vis-a-vis* the brahmana priests. Therefore, the non-brahmana priests or the descendants of the original tribal priests of the pre-Hinduized shrine/deity felt threatened and made an even more energetic effort to get themselves Hinduized and thereby to protect their interest and position at the shrine. As a part of that effort they created their own origin myth which sought to establish their closeness to the shrine/deity concerned and also their superiority in several different ways — though not in the *jati* ranking — and got the same incorporated and interwoven into the long existing *ksetra mahatmya* or *sthala purana* type of mythical tradition. As a result the folk version of the *ksetra mahatmya* or the *sthala purana* got restructured and modified.

Later after their Hinduization and absorption into the Hindu society, which was at best partial and not complete, sections of the non-brahmana priests of tribal origin wanted and attempted upward movement in the *jati*-ladder of the Hindu society and actively participated in the *jati* mobility.

But what was the driving force or motivation behind such an attempt at upward mobility in the *jati*-ladder? Was it a search for higher status or prestige? Was it the pecuniary benefit? Was it something else like the feeling of insecurity in the face of constant hostility and endeavour on the part of the brahmana priests to minimize their role, position and importance in the affairs of the deity and the cult? It appears that all these more or less inter-related factors together led to such an attempt at upward mobility in the *jati*-ladder by a sub-category of non-brahmana priests of tribal origin. In that connection it should be mentioned here that in the Hindu society, generally, the ranking in the *jati* hierarchy used to determine the prestige and status of an individual or a group of individuals. And this should be more so in case of the priests of a shrine/deity as the priestly profession has always been a highly competitive profession which has its own compulsion and priority and which generates its own tension. This was particularly so in the present case as it involved priests of different categories, brahmanas and non-brahmanas, originating from different ethnic stock. Further in a priestly profession the pecuniary benefit is closely related to the prestige and status of individual priests or groups of priests and is derived out of the same.

Next comes the question of the strategy adopted by a sub-category of the non-brahmana priests to realize their goal of upward movement in the *jati*-ladder. It appears that, among other things, the following means of cultural adaptions were made to play important roles in that process: (a) a new *jati* name and (b) a new origin myth. Firstly they assumed a completely new *jati* name — or rather a name for the sub-category of non-brahmana priests to which they themselves belonged — for themselves that endeavoured to indicate their independent identity as a category of priests, different from other non-brahmana priests of tribal origin and also as a new *jati*. This new name facilitated their upward movement in the *jati*-ladder indirectly. Secondly they created another origin myth which not only sought to authenticate and legitimize their independent status as a category of priests and as a new *jati* but also to establish their higher position in the *jati* ranking *vis-a-vis* the position of other non-brahmana priests of tribal origin. Further it even tried to demonstrate their proximity to the brahmana priests in the *jati* ranking (though it did not deny their tribal origin). This new origin myth was created by further restructuring and modifying the long existing but already restructured and modified *ksetra mahatmya* or *sthala purana* type of traditional account. Thus the new origin myth was directly responsible for their upward movement in the *jati*-ladder.

It may be mentioned here that firstly at the time of the Hinduization of the tribal shrine/deity, then at the time of the Hinduization of the original tribal worshipper-priests of the same tribal shrine/deity and finally at the time of the upward movement of a section of Hinduized descendants of the original tribal worshipper-priests in the *jati*-ladder there could have been some of kind of Brahmanic opposition which is not at all surprising. But, there are reasons to believe that, always another section of the brahmanas, for sectarian interests, supported nay welcomed the Hinduization of the shrine/deity as well as of the original tribal worshipper-priests and also the upward movement of the latter in the *jati*-ladder subsequently. It also appears that most probably the common people accepted the same without any opposition.

All that have been discussed above show how and why the Pujakaization type of *ksetra*-centred-Hinduization process operated in medieval Orissa and also perhaps elsewhere in India and how and why the original tribal priests of a tribal shrine/deity and their descendants were Hinduized and got absorbed into the Hindu society along with the Hinduization of same shrine/deity. This contradicts the image of an unchaging or static medieval society sometimes assumed by scholars. On the contrary it presents the picture of a very lively ever-changing dynamic society in which autochthonous tribes got constantly Hinduized and then participated in *jati*-mobility, in which forces and counter-forces constantly emerged and interacted generating, in turn, new forces and counter-forces to interact afresh.

Further the above discussion also demonstrates how the

traditional account, particularly the traditional account of *ksetra mahatmya* or *sthala purana* type, played an active and very significant role in the social dynamics of the primarily religion-centred medieval society facilitating Hinduization of the tribals and subsequently their participation in the *jati*-mobility which is generally not perceived or realized. In the process the traditional account got restructured and modified, sometimes even more than once, in order to be able to play this very definite and assigned role in the medieval social dynamics. Because of that very reason the traditional account in a way reflects and bears the picture of medieval social dynamics. Of course this reflection should not be confused with only the direct and passive reflection of medieval society which is generally assumed by the scholars. In other words the traditional account does not only reflect or bear the picture of the medieval society merely like a mirror. Because, unlike a mirror, it actively participated in the interaction of different forces and counter-forces in the medieval social dynamics which left its undeniably observable marks — even of the slightest stirrings and minutest movement of the same — on the body of the traditional account. And that is how the traditional account also reflects and bears the picture of medieval social dynamics indirectly which is much more important. Therefore, while reconstructing history of the medieval society, attempts should be made to find out the possible major as well as minor roles played by a traditional account in the interaction of different forces and counter-forces and in the process to discover and gather the indirect reflections of the medieval society in the same, very carefully and piecemeal. Then the separate pieces of the picture, thus gathered, must be put together as in the case of a jigsaw puzzle so that a correct and complete picture of the medieval society will ultimately emerge. It follows that in the reconstruction of the history of medieval society the importance and significance of the traditional account can never be minimized.

Thus a thorough study of the medieval social dynamics and particularly the process of the Pujakaization type of *ksetra-*

centred-Hinduization of the tribals and *jati* mobility and also the interesting and significant roles played by the *ksetra mahatmya* or *sthala purana* type of traditional account in the same processes can explain satisfactorily the apparently unbelievable and paradoxical phenomenon that the priests of tribal origin have been functioning for centuries at one of the most famous Hindu shrines, the temple of Lord Jagannatha at Puri, where the untouchables were denied entrance till 1948.

Appendix I

In the present work, except in direct quotations, the names of the persons, deities, texts, months in the Hindu calender, ceremonies, communities and some other words — most of the primary source materials being in Oriya — appear either in the Roman script as they are spelled in Oriya adopting the standard practices of transliteration minus the diacritical marks or in the anglicized forms as per the established convention. But in order to enable the readers to know exactly how some of these are spelled in Oriya and also to correlate — wherever possible — these names and words with the corresponding Sanskrit forms the requisite information has been supplied below in the following manner.

In Column I the names and the words have been given as they appear in the present work in alphabetical order; in Column II the spelling of the same in Oriya has been indicated within the square brackets and in Column III the corresponding Sanskrit forms have been given as per the standard practices of transliteration.

A. Names of the Persons, Deities, Texts, etc.

Column I	*Column II*	*Column III*
Anasara	[Aṇasara]	Anavasara
Balaram Das	[Baḷarāma Dāsa]	. . .
Bana Parba	[*Bana Parba*]	*Vana Parvan*
Basu	[Basu]	Vasu
Bhaba Samudra	[*Bhāba Samudra*]	*Bhāva Samudra*
Bhattarika	[Bhaṭṭārikā]	Bhaṭṭārikā
Bidyapati	[Bidyāpati]	Vidyāpati
Bisnu	[Bisṇu]	Viṣṇu

Column I	*Column II*	*Column III*
Bisva Basu	[Biśvā Basu]	Viśā Vasu
Brahma	[Brahmā]	Brahmā
Brahman	[Brāhmaṇa]	brāhmaṇa
Brahma Purana	[*Brahma Purāṇa*]	*Brahma Purāṇa*
Caitanya Caritamrt	[*Caitanya Caritāmṛta*]	*Caitanya Caritāmṛta*
Caitanya Mangal	[*Caitanya Maṅgaḷa*]	*Caitanya Mangala*
Casa	[Caṣā]	. . .
Chasa	[Caṣā]	. . .
Daita	[Daitā]	. . .
Daitya-nasana	[*Daitya-nāśana*]	. . .
Daitya-nisudana	[*Daitya-niṣūdana*]	. . .
Daksa Prajapati	[Dakṣa Prajāpati]	. . .
Dama Das	[Dāma Dāsa]	. . .
Damu Das	[Dāmu Dāsa]	. . .
Dandi Ramayana	[Dāṇḍi Rāmāyaṇa]	. . .
Daru Brahma Gita	[Dāru Brahma Gītā]	. . .
Desa Khanja	[Deśa Khanjā]	. . .
Deula Tola	[Deuḷa Toḷā]	. . .
Dinabandhu	[Dīnabandhu]	Dīnabandhu
Diti	[Diti]	Diti
Dvapara	[*Dvāparạ*]	*Dvāpara*
Gala	[Gāla]	. . .
Galaba	[Gālaba]	. . .
Gopi Tirtha Matha	[Gopī Tīrtha Maṭha]	. . .
Haribhakti Ratnabali	[*Haribhakti Ratnābaḷī*]	*HaribhaktiRatnāvalī*
Harivamsa	[Haribaṁśa]	Harivaṁśa
Indradyumna	[Indradyumna]	Indradyumna
Jagamohana Ramayana	[Jagamohana Rāmāyaṇa]	. . .
Jajati Kesari	[Jajāti Keśarī]	Yayāti Kesarī
Jara	[Jārā]	. . .
Karan	[Karaṇa]	. . .
Karmangi	[*Karmāṅgī*]	. . .

Column I	*Column II*	*Column III*
Khambesvari	[Khambeśvarī]	Stambheśvarī
Khandayat	[Khaṇḍāyata]	. . .
Khilamunda	[Khiḷāmuṇḍā]	. . .
Kriyayogasara	[*Kriyāyogasāra*]	. . .
Kr̥ṣṇa	[Kr̥ṣṇa]	Kr̥ṣṇa
Ksatriya	[Kṣatriya]	Kṣatriya
Lalita	[Laḷitā]	Lalitā
Madala Panji	[*Mādaḷā Pānjī*]	. . .
Madhava	[Mādhaba]	Mādhava
Magunia Das	[Māguṇiā Dāsa]	. . .
Mahabharata	[*Mahābhārata*]	*Mahābhārata*
Musali Parba	[*Muṣaḷī Parba*]	*Mauṣala Parvan*
Navakalevara	[*Nabakaḷebara*]	*Navakalevara*
Niladrimahodaya	[Nīḷādrimahodaya]	Nīlādrimaho-dayaḥ
Nilagiri	[Nīḷagiri]	Nīlagiri
Nila Madhava	[Nīḷa Mādhaba]	Nīla Mādhava
Nilambar Das	[Nīḷāmbara Dāsa]	. . .
Padma Purana	[*Padma Purāṇa*]	*Padma Purāṇa*
Pasupalaka	[Paśupāḷaka]	Puṣpālaka(?)
Pati Mahapatra	[Pati Mahāpātra]	. . .
Prapannamrta	[*Prapannāmr̥ta*]	*Prapannāmr̥ta*
Pujapanda	[*Pujāpaṇḍā*]	. . .
Rajabhoga	[*Rājabhoga*]	. . .
Ramanuja	[Rāmānuja]	Rāmānuja
R̥gveda	[*R̥gveda*]	*R̥gveda*
Rohini Kunda	[*Rohiṇī Kuṇḍa*]	*Rohiṇī Kuṇḍa*
Sabara	[Śabara]	Śavara
Sarala Das	[Sāraḷā Dāsa]	. . .
Sarala Mahabharata	[*Sāraḷā Mahābhārata*]	. . .
Satya	[*Satya*]	*Satya*
Saura	[Saurā]	Śavara
Savara	[Śabara]	Śavara
Savari Narayana	[Śabarī Nārāyaṇa]	Śavarī Nārāyaṇa

Column I	Column II	Column III
Sayana	[Sāyaṇa]	Sāyaṇa
Sisu Dama Das	[Śiśu Dāma Dāsa]	. . .
Sisu Krsna Das	[Śiśu Kṛṣṇa Dāsa]	. . .
Skanda Purana	[*Skanda Purāṇa*]	*Skanda Purāṇa*
Sora	[Saurā]	Śavara
Srīkṣetra Mahatmya	[*Srīkṣetra Mahatmya*]	*Srīkṣetra Mahatmya*
Sudha Suara	[Sudha Suāra]	. . .
Sudra	[Ṣudra]	Śūdra
Vaisya	[Baiśya]	Vaiśya
Visnu	[Biṣṇu]	Viṣṇu

B. Other Words

Column I	Column II	Column III
acarya	[*ācārya*]	*ācārya*
anuloma	[*anuloma*]	*anuloma*
asura	[*asura*]	*asura*
bamsa	[*baṃśa*]	*vaṃśa*
brahmana	[*brāhmaṇa*]	*brāhmaṇa*
daitya	[*daitya*]	*daitya*
dayita	[*dayita*]	*dayita*
debata	[*debatā*]	*devatā*
devata	[*debatā*]	*devatā*
devata pati	[*debatā pati*]	*devatā pati*
dharma	[*dharma*]	*dharma*
dharma sastra	[*dharma śāstra*]	*dharma śāstra*
gotra	[*gotra*]	*gotra*
ista devata	[*iṣṭa debatā*]	*īṣṭa devatā*
janapada	[*janapada*]	*janapada*
jati	[*jāti*]	*jāti*
karana	[*karaṇa*]	. . .
khandayt	[*khaṇḍāyata*]	. . .
ksatriya	[kṣatriya]	kṣatriya

ksetra	*[kṣetra]*	*kṣetra*
Column I	Column II	Column III
ksetra mahatmya	*[kṣetra māhātmya]*	*kṣetra māhātmya*
mangalaropana	*maṅgaḷārpaṇa*	*[maṅgalāropaṇa]*
mitra	*[mitra]*	*mitra*
mrtyubhoja	*[mr̥tyubhoja]*	*mr̥tyubhoja*
nayaka	*[nāyaka]*	*nāyaka*
pahandi	*[pahaṇḍi]*	. . .
pujaka	*[pūjaka]*	*pūjaka*
punya	*[puṇya]*	*puṇya*
purana	*[purāṇa]*	*purāṇa*
raksasa	*[rākṣasa]*	*rākṣasa*
rastra devata	*[rāṣṭra devatā]*	*rāṣṭra devatā*
ratha	*[ratha]*	*ratha*
rauta	*[rāuta]*	. . .
sebaka	*[sebaka]*	*sevaka*
sevaka	*[sevaka]*	*sevaka*
snana	*[snāna]*	*snāna*
sthala purana	*[sthaḷa purāṇa]*	*sthala purāṇa*
suara	*[suāra]*	*sūpakāra*
suara	*[suāra]*	. . .
tirtha	*[tīrtha]*	*tīrtha*
vamsa	*[baṃśa]*	*vaṃśa*
vara	*[bara]*	*vara*
varna	*[barṇa]*	*varṇa*
yatra	*[jātrā]*	*yātrā*
yuga	*[juga]*	*yuga*

Appendix II

New Direction of Research in Medieval Orissan History

A Study in Methodology

IF in the last quarter of the twentieth-century India, which the constitution declares and is repeatedly claimed to be a secular state, the religion and its representatives could play very important roles and could exert tremendous influence on its society and polity — the facts are so numerous and so self-obvious that citing example is almost unnecessary — one is tempted to imagine that in the medieval Orissa, where religion and politics got almost completely mixed and mingled together, the representatives of the religion were immensely powerful. As the society in medieval Orissa, in general, was religion oriented the representatives of religion could shape the thought-process and influence the actions of people in almost every sphere.

In medieval Orissa, the population of which has always been predominantly Hindu, the most prominent among the representatives of religion were:

(i) the brahmanas, whose exclusive business was to compile, quote and interpret the scriptures, their leaders hailing generally from the different *sasana* villages or agraharas established near about Puri and Cuttack by the kings with large endowments of land in their favour;

This paper was presented in the Seminar on Society and Culture in Medieval Orissa held in May, 1979 organised by the Department of History, Khallikote College, Berhampur.

(ii) the Priests of the different deities among whom really the most influential were the priests of Lord Jagannatha at Puri who was made the *rastra devata* or the state deity during the medieval period; and

(iii) the Saints belonging to different Hindu sects and sub-sects among whom were also included the devotees of different deities, the devotees of Lord Jagannatha being the most prominent among them.

Each of these three groups consisted of several sub-groups and there are evidences leading to the existence of intra-group rivalries and feuds among them. But these sub-groups normally patched up their differences and their members behaved unitedly as members of one single homogeneous group when fighting for superiority and benefits with other group/groups. A study on their inter-group relationship as well as their relationship with the king, head of the political establishment and the chief of the political-military power structure in medieval Orissa, promises to be highly interesting in itself and that is one of the aims of this paper which has so far been ignored by the contemporary scholars. Further, it is hoped that, the results will facilitate a better understanding of the medieval Orissan society; will be useful in developing an insight into the interplay of different forces and counter-forces in it and will also be useful in many other fields of research.

As for this period of Orissan history only scanty information is available. It is proposed here to depend mainly on the legendary/semi-legendary and mythical/semi-mythical traditional accounts as source materials which is another departure from the present practice.

It may be mentioned here that as a further deviation from the earlier practice, in the present paper the question, whether a particular traditional account has any or substantial historical basis or not leading to its complete acceptance or rejection as a source material of history has been subordinated to the questions: what purpose and whose interest it did serve and what message it transmitted to the people in general as that will serve our purpose better. As for example there may not be any historical basis behind the traditional account (which, incidentally, is a sub-tradition or sub-part of the famous Kanci-Kaveri tradition of Orissa) that one Godabara Misra, the preceptor of Gajapati Purushottam Dev, the emperor of Orissa (1467-98) could cause a sudden flood in the river Godavari by *tantrik* rites and thus could prevent the utter defeat that awaited Orissan army on its way back from the victorious campaign at Kanci when the king of Kanci almost fell on it with a freshly gathered but large and superior force and as a result was awarded the title Godavari *vardhan*. But does it mean nothing at all? Is this tradition completely worthless in the reconstruction of the history of Orissa? Is this devoid of any significance at all? Perhaps this tradition sought to create an impression in the medieval Orissan society that the brahmanas were quite powerful and could do and undo things and as a result made the people more respectful towards the brahmanas. Perhaps it also sought to send the signal that the brahmanas supported the kings and there was no dissension between the brahmanas on the one hand and the kings on the other. Or perhaps it sought to persuade the people at large that the brahmanas could still play an important role in military affairs as earlier in the Ganga period when the brahmanas generally led the imperial army. This appears to be the case as the same Godabara Misra successfully pursued also the goal of writing a military treatise named *Harihara Caturanga* which only betrays his utter ignorance of military knowledge and field experience as it treats the chariot as a wing of the army in the classical tradition (i.e., *Caturanga bala*) though by that time chariot had become obsolete in Indian warfare for centuries.

Anyway after the traditional accounts are subjected to such questions as mentioned above one can hope to draw a relatively more complete and more satisfactory picture of the religion oriented medieval society. This is especially so in case of the mythical/semi-mythical traditional accounts as these have a very special place in every ancient and medieval religion and as such are likely to throw much light on some dark corners which otherwise may remain enveloped in darkness.

It may be mentioned here that traditional accounts may originate either as written or as oral tradition. Sometimes some traditions originating as oral traditions may later get written down during the medieval period itself. But some of the oral traditions may continue to remain oral for centuries till they are finally collected and written down by scholars in modern times. Sometimes even, though rarely, a tradition may originate as a written tradition but later the written form may get lost while it may continue to be transmitted in oral form commencing with the people who once read the same in the written form.

As the major concern of this paper is primarily to provide an example of a new direction of research no great effort will be made here for an exhaustive collection of written as well as oral traditions pertaining to the subject. Instead reference will be made to only few well-known and easily available written traditions. These traditions originated either as written traditions or as oral traditions which subsequently got written down in the medieval period itself. It is further proposed to confine the scope of the following study to the later medieval period especially to the period between the fifteenth and the eighteenth centuries.

The traditional accounts which are proposed to be used as source material for the present study may come under the following four major classes according to their source of origin and medium of tranmission. In other words the traditional accounts will be classified according to the groups representing the religious and/or political establishments which created these traditional accounts in the first place and then preserved and transmitted them in late medieval Orissa:

CLASS 1: THE BRAHMANIC TRADITIONS

Under which comes *Cakada Basana*, which has been published edited by Sudhakar Pattanayak, 36 verses in the last canto of *Bhakti Bhagavata* by Jivadeva Acharya, selected portions from the published historical work entitled *Utkala Itihasara Eka Ajnata Adhyaya* by Chakradhar Mahapatra, etc.

CLASS 2: THE PRIESTLY TRADITIONS

Under which comes *Madala Panji* (*Rajabhoga Itihasa*) which has been published edited by A.B. Mohanty, *Odradesa-Rajavamsavali* which has been published edited by K.C. Mishra or *Kataka Rajavamsavali* which has been published edited by G.C. Tripathi and H. Kulke etc. (These traditions may appear to be the Royal Traditions from their names or otherwise. But for our purpose they are the Priestly Traditions.)

CLASS 3: THE SAINTLY TRADITIONS

Under which comes *Ramanuja Divya Caritai*, *Prapannamrta* by Anantacarya, *Bhaktamala* by Candradatta, *Caitanya Mangal* by Jayanand, *Jagannatha Caritamrta* by Dibakar Das, *Dardhyata Bhakti* by Rama Das, *Bedantasara Gupta Gita*, *Bhaba Samudra*, *Bata Abakasa*, *Panasa Cori* and others ascribed to the authorship of Balaram Das, *Deula Tola*, a group of texts written by a number of authors, etc.

CLASS 4: THE ROYAL TRADITIONS

Under which comes *Gangavamsanucaritam* a *campu kavyam* by Vasudeva Ratha Somayaji, *Nagasagotranrpa Vamsanucaritam*, the imperial Ganga *prasasti* found in a number of copper-plate inscriptions issued by the Ganga kings of Orissa, etc.

And each of these four classes of traditional accounts can be studied in terms of the types of motifs or thematic-types that are found in them establishing, directly or indirectly, the superiority of one particular group *vis-a-vis* with the other group/groups and also showing its relationship with the other group/groups. From a preliminary analysis the following two major types of motifs or major thematic types (each in turn consisting of several sub-types) have been discovered :

Thematic-type No. 1
(in which a deity, preferably Lord Jagannatha, figures and plays an important role)

SUB-TYPES

1.1. The deity favours group A thereby establishing its superiority.

1.2. The deity supports group A against group B in a test of strength.

1.2.1. The deity supports group A against group B and group A wins in a test of strength.

1.2.2. One deity supports group A and another deity supports group B in a test of strength in which group A wins.

It may be mentioned here that a deity is made to play a role mostly in the Saintly and Priestly traditions but rarely if ever in Brahmanic or Royal traditions.

Thematic-type No. 2
(in which no deity figures or is made to play a role)

SUB-TYPES

2.1. Group A is complimented and rewarded/denounced and punished.

2.2. Group A demonstrates its power and establishes superiority *vis-a-vis* other group/groups.

2.3. Group A is favourable towards group B.

2.4. Group A surrenders its rights/prerogatives in favour of group B.

2.5. Group A humbles group B in a test of strength.

2.6. Group A comes to grief as it did not behave judiciously or properly with group B.

2.7. Group A supports group B against group C.

It should be made very clear at this point that in any one class of tradition (for example in the Brahmanic or Priestly tradition) both the major types of motifs or the major thematic-types (with their sub-types) may be found which is quite natural. But that does not, of course, mean that both the major types of motifs or major thematic-types must necessarily be found in each and every class of traditional accounts. Similarly more than one class of traditional accounts may use the same thematic-type or sub-type. In other words the same thematic-type or even the sub-type may be found in different classes of tradition. Therefore each of these thematic-types or sub-types may have variant forms depending on the actual group occupying the slots A, B or C.

Now a sketch of the thematic-types and sub-types with their variant forms found in each class of traditions may be given.

The Brahmanic Tradition

1.1. Lord Jagannatha favours the kings (Kanci-Kaveri tradition as reported in *Cakada Basana*); Lord Jagannatha favours the priests (in the same tradition as found in Kanci Kaberi by Purusottam Das and also in *Madala Panji*).

1.2. The deity Nrsimha Natha supports the brahmanas against the saints (as reported in *Cakada Basana*); A number of deities support the saints against the brahmanas (in the same text).

2.1. The kings are mentioned most respectfully (in *Cakada Basana* and also in *Bhakti Bhagavata*); The Brahmanas are mentioned most respectfully (in *Cakada Basana* and also in *Bhakti Bhagavata*).

2.1 The kings are criticised (in *Utkala Itihasara Eka Ajnata Adhyaya*).

2.5. The kings humiliate the Brahmanas (thereby creating antipathy towards the kings in *Utkala Itihasara Eka Ajnata Adhyaya*).

2.6. The kings come to grief as they did not behave properly with the brahmanas (in the 9th verse of the last canto of *Bhakti Bhagavata* and also in *Utkala Itihasara Eka Ajnata Adhyaya*).

2.7. The kings support the saints against the brahmanas (in Caitanya episode in *Utkala Itihasara Eka Ajnata Adyaya*).

The Priestly Tradition

1.1.1. Lord Jagannatha favours the kings (Chodaganga, Kapilendra and Purusottama's accession as recorded in *Madala Panji*).

1.1.2. Lord Jagannatha favours the saints (the blind Daita Dasa episode as recorded in *Madala Panji*).

1.2.1.1. Lord Jagannatha supports the priests against the kings (Dasa Mahasuara tradition as recorded in *Madala Panji*; *Bala dhupa* tradition in *Madala Panji*).

1.2.1.2. Lord Jagannatha supports the priests against the saints (setback for Acarya, i.e., Ramanuja as recorded in *Madala Panji*)

2.1.1. The saints are mentioned respectfully (*Caitanya*, *Pancasakhas* and blind Daita Dasa traditions as recorded in *Madala Panji*).

2.1.2. The kings are mentioned respectfully (in *Madala Panji*).

2.1.2. The kings are criticised (in *Madala Panji*).

2.2. The brahmanas demonstrate their extraordinary power (in Candracora Bahinipati, Tucha Mathia Misra and

Godavari Mahapatra traditions in *Madala Panji*).

2.3.1. The kings are favourable towards the priests (king Anangabhima Deva appointed a good number of priests in the temple of Jagannatha as recorded in *Madala Panji*).

2.3.2. The kings are favourable towards the saints (*Caitanya* and *Pancasakhas* as mentioned in *Madala Panji*).

2.3.3. The brahmanas are favourable towards the kings (flooding of the river Godavari episode in the famous Kanci-Kaveri tradition recorded in *Madala Panji*).

2.5. The kings humiliate the brahmanas evoking antipathy of the brahmanas towards the kings (Cakra Pratap of the Bhoi dynasty in *Madala Panji*).

2.6. The kings come to grief as they did not behave properly with the brahmanas (the fall of Kesari dynasty as recorded in *Madala Panji*).

2.7. The kings support the saints against the priests (Purusottama Deva of Surya dynasty supporting one Acarya against the priests as recorded in *Madala Panji*.)

The Saintly Tradition

1.1. Lord Jagannatha favours the saints (Salabeg sambada in *Dardhyata Bhakti*.

1.2.1.1. Lord Jagannatha supports the saints against the kings (Balaram Das tradition as found in *Bhaba Samudra*, Bandhu Mahanti sambad found in *Dardhyata Bhakti*, the superiority test between the *Gita Govinda* by Jayadev and its royal imitation as recorded in *Bhaktamala* by Candradatta and in *Dardhyata Bhakti*, etc.).

1.2.1.2. Lord Jagannatha supports the saints against the brahmanas (Balaram Das tradition as found in *Bedantasara Gupta Gita*).

1.2.1.3. Lord Jagannatha supports the saints against the priests (Balaram Das sambad in *Dardhyata Bhakti*, Dasia Bauri sambad in the same work, etc.).

1.2.1.4. Lord Jagannatha supports the priests against the kings (Tilicha Mahapatra sambad in *Dardhyata Bhakti*).

1.2.1.5. Lord Jagannatha supports the priests against the saints (Ramanuja's setback in Puri recorded in Ramanuja *Divya Caritai* and *Prapannamrta*).

2.3. The kings are favourable towards the priests (King Indradyumna seeks a favour from Lord Jagannatha that nobody should ever find any fault with the temple servants as mentioned in *Deula Tola* by Magunia Das and *Daru Brahma* by Dama Das).

2.4. The kings surrender their own right in favour of the priests (King Indradyumna seeks a very strange favour from Lord Jagannatha that his *vamsa* or line be extinct lest his descendants should claim ownership over the temple of Jagannatha as mentioned in various *Deula Tola* texts).

2.5. The kings are humbled by the saints (traditions regarding Jagannatha Das as found in *Jagannatha Caritamrta* by Dibakara Das).

2.6.1. The kings support the brahmanas against the saints (as found in *Bedantasara Gupta Gita* ascribed to Balaram Das).

2.6.2. The kings support the saints against the priests (Ramanuja's set- back at Puri as mentioned in Ramanuja *Divya Caritai* and *Prapannamrta*).

The Royal Tradition

1.1. Lord Jagannatha favours the kings (as mentioned in the imperial Ganga *prasasti* found in a number of copper-plate inscriptions).

2.2. The kings demonstrate their power (as mentioned in the imperial Ganga *prasasti* found in a number of copper-plate inscriptions).

2.3. The kings are favourable towards the brahmanas (as found in the Catesvara temple inscription of Anangabhima III of the Ganga dynasty).

Comparing the different thematic types and sub-types of the traditional accounts and their variations occurring in the different classes of traditions the following tentative conclusions may be drawn here:

1.a The saints considered the brahmanas, the kings and the priests their antagonists in that order, i.e., their grievances against the priests were the least and against the brahmanas the most.

1.b The priests considered the kings and the saints their antagonists in that order. It is significant that they did not consider the brahmanas as their antagonist. In other words they did not apprehend any danger from the brahmanas. Of course they did not like the brahmanas very much and were not very respectful towards them. Nevertheless they did not like the brahmanas to be humiliated by the kings. (It may be remembered here that a dominant section of the priests were brahmanas).

1.c The brahmanas considered the saints as their antagonists. They also had some grievances against the kings. (Perhaps they expected the kings to be even more generous towards them.) It seems the brahmanas had least grievance against the priests.

1.d The kings, it seems, considered none of these groups their antagonists, i.e., they had nothing to fear from any of these groups. They were of course more generous towards the brahmanas. They, perhaps, wanted to have brahmanas as their allies in the smooth administration of their kingdom. (Though the kings were not afraid of either the saints or the priests they interfered in the affairs of the saints and the priests from time to time and even at times harassed them.)

2.a It seems the saints and the priests were close to each other though they quarrelled among themselves occasionally. The saints were more respectful towards the priests than the priests were towards them. Though the saints did not consider the priests in any way inferior to them the priests, it appears, considered themselves a little superior. The saints made common cause with the priests whenever the priests were in conflict with the kings and even brought pressure on the latter to surrender to the preists as far as the administration of the temple of Jagannatha is concerned. Similarly they also resisted the attempts of the brahmanas to meddle in the affairs of the priests.

2.b The kings and the brahmanas were also every close to each other.

2.c The priests and the brahmanas never came to any conflict with each other.

2.d The saints and the brahmanas quarrelled from time to time.

2.e The kings and the priests also quarrelled from time to time. But at the same time the priests supported the accession of the kings to the throne and also tried to legitimize the same.

The above conclusions are only tentative in nature as only the easily available and written traditional accounts have been used as source material in the present paper and are subject to revision. Further the preceding analysis may seem over-simplification of a very complex problem as the approach has been completely synchronic. In other words it has almost been assumed as if the time stood still and did not move at all in the whole of the medieval period when in fact traditional accounts first emerged, then were propagated and finally were written down at different points of time and got modified in the process. Not only that it has also been assumed as if different traditional accounts emerged almost at the same time and there was no time-gap among them. This approach may not depict the whole picture. On the other hand this approach may lead us to conclusions which are apparently contradictory to each other. An example may be given here.

There is a traditional account recorded in two medieval texts, *Bhaba Samudra*, ascribed to the sixteenth-century saint-poet Balaram Das and *Dardhyata Bhakti* (the 14th *adhyaya*, Balaram Das sambad, of the latter) by the eighteenth-century poet Ram Das. The tradition belongs to the class of the Saintly Tradition. According to the tradition once, during the car-festival, Balaram Das, the saint and devotee of Lord Jagannatha, went up the car (i.e., the chariot) of Lord Jagannatha in order to pay his respects to the Lord. But, as he had not observed the rules of purity, he was driven out of the car, insulted and humiliated. According to the *Bhaba Samudra* version of the tradition he was driven out of the car by the king whereas according to the *Dardhyata Bhakti* version he was driven out of the car by the temple-priests. Thus humiliated the grief-stricken saint-devotee went to the sea shore and there built three cars out of the sand and invoked Lord Jagannatha to come there. The Lord, pleased with his devotion, came there along with his elder brother and sister leaving behind the real cars and remained in the sand cars. As the deities left the cars the same could not be moved in spite of the best efforts made by the persons who were in charge of pulling the cars. Even the king engaging all the resources at his command was not able to get the cars moved an inch. Then the Lord appeared before the king in a dream and told him the reason behind such unusual phenomenon. He further told the king that person/persons responsible for the humiliation of the saint-devotee — i.e., the king himself according to the *Bhaba Samudra* version but the temple-priests according to the *Dardhyata Bhakti* version of the tradition — must go most humbly to the saint-devotee, apologize to him and bring him back to the real cars after which only the cars could be pulled and moved and the festival could be held. When the command of the Lord was obeyed the cars did move and the festival was held.

Therefore the same thematic type and even the same thematic sub-type could be found in both the versions of the tradition (i.e., the thematic sub-type 1.2.1.) which is not at all surprising. In other words in this tradition the deity — in the present case Lord Jagannatha — supports group A against the group B and group A wins in a test of strength. But though slot A is occupied by the group *Saints* in both the versions of the tradition, which is quite natural in a Saintly Tradition, the slot B is occupied by the group *Kings* in one of the versions (i.e., the *Bhaba Samudra* version) and the group *Priests or Temple-priests* in the other version (i.e., the *Dardhyata Bhakti* version) of the same. Thus there is a contradiction. This contradiction can be resolved if we take into consideration the fact that the texts belong to two different points of time which reflect the change of position and attitude of the group Saints which was primarily responsible for the creation of the tradition and subsequently its transmission.

Therefore the synchronic approach alone cannot give us a complete and correct picture and a combination of both the synchronic and diachronic approaches seems rather necessary which can bring us nearer to the truth. Similarly the frequency of occurrence of a particular thematic type/sub-type and its variations may be quite significant which should be taken into consideration while analysing the traditional accounts. But as has been explained earlier the primary purpose of this paper is not to arrive at any definite conclusion regarding the relationship that existed among the different religious and political-military groups in medieval Orissa but to highlight a new direction of research. It is now hoped that the primary purpose of this paper has been achieved.

Bibliography

A. Primary Sources

Bhaba Samudra, by Balaram Das, compiled by Govinda Rath, 1910, Cuttack: Arunoday Press. Oriya.

Caitanya Caritamrt, by Krsna Das Kaviraj. Bengali.

Caitanya Mangal, by Jayananda, ed. by B.B. Majumdar and S. Mukhopadhyay, 1971, Calcutta: Asiatic Society. Bengali.

Daru Brahma, by Dama Das, unpublished manuscript. Paper Copy Orissa Research Project. Oriya.

Desa Kharja, unpublished manuscript bearing no name procured from Puri. It seems to be a copy of *Desakharja* section *Madala Panji* or the Records of the Jagannatha temple, Puri. Paper copy Orissa Research Project. Oriya.

Deula Tola, by Magunia Das, unpublished palm-leaf manuscript in the possession of K.C. Sahu, retired Professor of Oriya, Utkal University, Paper Copy. Oriya.

Deula Tola, by (Sisu) Krsna Das.

a .1950, Cuttack: Dasarathi Pustakalaya. Oriya.

b. 1953, Cuttack: Kohinoor Press. Oriya.

c. ———, Cuttack: Prabhati Press. Oriya.

Gangavamsanucaritam (*campu kavyam*) by Vasudeva Ratha

Somayaji, ed. by Pramila Mishra, 1979, Bhubaneswar: Directorate of Tourism & Cultural Affairs. Sanskrit.

Gopi Tirtha Matha Manuscript, unpublished manuscript preserved in the Gopi Tirtha Matha, Bhubaneswar. Paper Copy Orissa Research Project. (This is very close to, perhaps a different version of, the *Desakhanja* manuscript mentioned above.) Oriya.

Karmangi, the complete title is "Sri Sri Purusottama Jaganntha Mandira Sebaka Khatani Nijoga Karmangi", i.e., the record of the services of the temple-servants of the temple of Purushottama-Jagannatha, ed. by Siddheswar Mahapatra, in: *Anama Sankalana*— 19, 1983, Cuttack: G.B. Mahanty. Oriya.

Kataka Rajavamsavali, ed. by G.C. Tripathi and Hermann Kulke, 1987, Allahabad: Vohra Publishers & Distributors. Sanskrit.

Madala Panji, ed. by A.B. Mohanty, 1940, Cuttack: Prachi Samity. Oriya.

Odradesa Rajavamsavali, ed. by B. Panda, 1983, Bhubaneswar: Institute of Orissa Culture. Sanskrit.

Record-of-Rights, Prepared under the Puri Shri Jagannatha Temple (Administration) Act (Orissa Act XIV of 1952) and Rules made thereunder. Published in the Orissa Gazzette Extraordinary:
Part I No. 101, May 7, 1955.
Part III (iii) Vol. 1, No. 293, Oct. 14, 1956.
Vol. 2, 1956.
Vol. 3, No. 152, June 27, 1956.
Vol. 4, No. 203, Sept. 3, 1956.

Sarala Mahabharata (Asvamedha, Musali O Svargarohana Parba), by Sarala Das, ed. by A.B. Mohanty, 1970,

Bhubaneswar: Department of Cultural Affairs, Government of Orissa. Oriya.

Sarala Mahabharata (Bana Parba), by Sarala Das, ed. by A.B. Mohanty, 1970, Bhubaneswar: Department of Cultural Affairs, Government of Orissa. Oriya.

Sriksetra Mahatmya ba Deula Tola, by Damu Das, 1323 Sal. Kanthi: Nihar Press. Oriya in Bengali script.

B. Secondary Sources

Acharya, Paramanand, 1969a, *Studies in Orissan History, Archaeology and Archives*, Cuttack: Cuttack Students' Store.

———, 1969b, *Odisara Pratnatattva O Anyanya Prabandha*, Bhubaneswar: Orissa Sahitya Akademi. Oriya.

Acharya, Pyarimohan, 1925, *Orissara Itihasa*, Cuttack: The Utkal Sahitya Press, (First edition, 1879). Oriya.

Appadurai, Arjun, 1977, "Kings, Sects and Temples in South India", in: *The Indian Economic and Social History Review*, XIV No. 1, pp. 47-73.

Bhowmick, P.K., 1961, "Artificial Relationship in Midnapur", in: *Man in India*, 41/2, pp. 111-13.

Chakravarti, M.M., 1895, "Two copper-plate inscriptions of the King Nrsimha-deva IV of Orissa", in: *JASB*, LXIV Part I, No. 2, pp. 128-54.

———, 1898a, "The date of the Jagannatha Temple in Puri, Orissa", in: *JASB*, LXVII, No. 4, pp. 328-31.

———, 1898b, "Notes on the language and literature of Orissa", Parts III and IV in: *JASB*, LXVII, No. 4, pp. 332-86.

Chand, R.P., 1927, "Notes from the Madala Panji— (Muhammadan

Conquest of Orissa)", in: *Journal of the Bihar and Orissa Research Society*, XIII/I, pp. 10-27.

Chaudhuri, B., 1964, "Sora", in: *Adibasi*, 1963-64, No.3, pp. 101-06.

Dash, G.N., 1976, "The King and the Priests: An Analysis of a Gita Gobinda Tradition", in: *Visva Bharati Quarterly*, 40/3, pp. 227-46.

———, 1978a, "The Evolution of the Priestly Power: The Gangavamsa Period", in: *The Cult of Jagannatha and the Regional Tradition of Orissa*, by A. Eschmann, H. Kulke and G.C. Tripathi (eds.) 1978. pp. 157-68.

———, 1978b, The "Evolution of the Priestly Power: The Suryavamsa Period", in: *The Cult of Jagannatha and the Regional Tradition of Orissa*, by A. Eschmann, H. Kulke and G.C. Tripathi (eds.) 1978, pp. 209-71.

———, 1979, *Janasruti Kanci Kaberi*, Berhampur: Pustaka Bhandar. Oriya.

———, 1982, "Janasruti O' Samajika Itihasa", in: *The Jhankar*, 34/4, pp. 337-46. Oriya. Reproduced in: *Dr. Kahnu Caran Misranka sasti purtti upalakse Abhinandan Grantha* (*K.C. Mishra Felicitation Volume*) by G. Bal, *et al.* (eds.) 1983: Cuttack: Tara Tatini Book Store.

———, 1985, "Janasruti O' Itihasa: Patita Pabana Jagannatha", in: *The Jhankar*, 37/6, pp. 475-87. Oriya.

———, 1988," Sarala Mahabharata O Itihasa", in: *Esana*, XVII, pp. 1-25. Oriya.

Das, Pandit Nilakanth, 1967," Odia Sahityara Krama Parinama, vol. 1 and 2", in: *Nilakantha Granthabali*, vol. 3, 1967, Cuttack, Students' Store. Oriya.

Das, Surya Narayan, 1966, *Odia Sahityara Itihasa*, Vol. 3,

Cuttack: Grantha Mandirs. Oriya.

——, 1967, *Jagannatha Mandira O' Jagannatha Tattva*, Cuttack: Friends Publishers. Oriya.

Dhal, U.N., 1992, "Sacred Ksetras of Orissa", in: *Utkal Historical Research Journal*, III pp. 121-24.

Eschmann, Anncharlott, 1978a, "Hinduization of Tribal Deities of Orissa: The Sakta and Saiva Typology", in: *The Cult of Jagannatha and the Regional Tradition of Orissa*, by A. Eschmann, H. Kulke and G.C. Tripathi (eds.), 1978, pp. 79-97.

——, 1878b," The Vaisnava Typology of Hinduization and the Origin of Jagannatha", in: *The Cult of Jagannatha and the Regional Tradition of Orissa*, by A. Eschmann, H. Kulke and G.C. Tripathi (eds.) 1978, pp. 99-117.

——, 1978c, "Prototypes of the Navakalevara Ritual and their Relation to Jagannatha Cult", in: *The Cult of Jagannatha and the Regional Tradition of Orissa*, by A. Eschmann, H. Kulke and G.C. Tripathi (eds.) 1978, pp. 265-83.

Eschmann, A., Kulke, H. and Tripathi, G.C., 1978, "The Formation of the Jagannatha Triad", in: *The Cult of Jagannatha and the Regional Tradition of Orissa*, by A. Eschmann, H. Kulke and G.C. Tripathi (eds.) 1978, pp. 169-96.

Eschmann, A., Kulke, H. and Tripathi, G.C. (eds)

——, 1978, *The Cult of Jagannatha and the Regional Tradition of Orissa*, New Delhi: Manohar Publications.

Fleet, J.F., 1894/95, "Records of the Somavamsi Kings of Katak", in *EI*, III/47, pp. 323-59.

Geib, Ruprecht, 1975, *Indradyumna Legende. Ein beitrag zur Geschichte des Jagannatha Kultes*, Wiesbaden: Steiner Verlag.

Hockett, C.F., 1970, *A Course in Modern Linguistics*, New Delhi: Oxford and IBH Publishing Co. (First Published 1958, The MacMillan Company).

Hunter, W.W., 1872, *Orissa*, Vol. 1, London: Smith, Elder & Co.

Jacobi, Hermann, 1971, "Daitya", in: *Encyclopaedia of Religion and Ethics*, Vol. 4, by J. Hastings *et al.* (eds.) 1971, Edinburgh: T. & T. Clark. (First Published 1911).

Kanaka Durga, P.S. and Sudhakar Reddy, Y.A., "Kings, Temples and Legitimation of Autochthonous Communities. A Case Study of a South Indian Temple", in: *Journal of the Economic and Social History of the Orient*, XXXV, pp. 145-66.

Kane, P.V., 1941, *History of Dharmasastra*, Vol. 2, Part I. Poona: Bhandarkar Oriental Research Institute.

Kulke, Hermann, 1976, "Kshatriyaization and Social Change. A Study in Orissan Setting", in: *Aspects of Change in India: Studies in Honour of Prof. G.S. Ghurye*, by S.D. Pillai (ed.) Bombay, 1976, pp. 398-409.

———, 1978a, "Royal Temple Policy and the Structure of Medieval Hindu Kingdom", in: *The Cult of Jagannatha and the Regional Tradition of Orissa*, by A. Eschmann, H. Kulke and G.C. Tripathi (eds.) 1978, pp. 125-37.

———, 1978b, "Early Royal Patronage of the Jagannatha Cult". in: *The Cult of Jagannatha and the Regional Tradition of Orissa*, by A. Eschmann, H. Kulke and G.C. Tripathi (eds.), 1978, pp. 139-55.

———, 1978c, "Juggernaut under British Supremacy and the Resurgence of the Khurda — Rajas as Rajas of Puri", in: *The Cult of Jagannatha and the Regional Tradition of Orissa*, by A. Eschamann, H. Kulke and G.C. Tripathi (eds.) 1978, pp. 345-57.

——, 1979, *Jagannatha Kult and Gajapati-Königtum*, Weisbaden: Franz Steiner Verlag Gmb H.

——, 1981, "King Anangabhima III, the Veritable Founder of the Gajapati Kingship and of the Jagannatha Trinity at Puri", in: *Journal of the Royal Asiatic Society*, 1981, No. 1, pp. 26-39.

——, 1984," Tribal Deities at Princely Courts. The Feudatory Rajas of Central Orissa and their Tutelary Deities", in: *Folkways in Religion: Gods, Spirits and Men*, by S. Mahapatra (ed.) 1984, pp. 13-24. Cuttack: Institute of Oriental and Orissan Studies.

——, 1987a, "Uberlegungen zu den Quellen der Tempelchroniken der Madala Panji Puris", in: *Hinduisms und Buddhismus, Festschrift fur Ulrich Schneider*, ed. by H. Falk, Freiburg, 1987, pp. 173-207.

——,1987b," The Chronicles and the Temple Records of the Madala Panji of Puri—A Reassessment of the Evidence", in: *The Indian Archives*, XXXVI/1 (January-June) pp. 1-24.

Kunar, D.C. (ed.), 1977, *Orissa District Gazetteers*: Puri, 1977, Bhubaneswar: Gazetteer Unit, Department of Revenue, Govt. of Orissa.

Lehmann, Winfred P., 1975, *Historical Linguistics: An Introduction*, New Delhi: Oxford and IBH Publishing Co. (First edition 1962, Holt Rinehart and Winston, Inc. New York).

Mahapatra, C., 1969, *Utkala Itihasara Eka Ajnata Adhyaya*, Cuttack: Friends Publishers.

——, 1982, "Mo Jibana Katha", in: *The Jhankar*, 34/3, pp. 259ff. Oriya.

Mahapatra, K.N., 1969, *Khurudha Itihasa*, Bhubaneswar: Published by the author. Oriya.

——, 1973, *Devotional Reference to Jagannath in the Old Oriya Literature*, (Type Script. Orissa Research Project).

Mahapatra, L.K., 1973, "Ritual Kinship in Orissa", in: *Bulletin of the Deccan College Research Institute*, XXXI, pp. 89-105.

Mandelbaum, David, G., 1972, *Society in India*, Bombay: Popular Prakashan, (First edition, 1970, University of California Press, U.S.A.).

Mansinha, Mayadhar, 1962, *History of Oriya Literature*, New Delhi: Sahitya Akademi.

Mishra, K.C., 1971, *The Cult of Jagannath*, Calcutta: Firma K.L. Mukhopadhyay.

Mishra, Krupasindhu, 1926, *Utkal Itihasa*, Cuttack and Puri: Sri Akula Mishra Kavyatirtha, General Manager, Cuttack Trading Company.

Mitra, R.L., 1961, *Antiquities of Orissa*, Vol. I. Calcutta: Indian Studies: Past & Present. (First published 1876).

——, 1963, *Antiquities of Orissa*, Vol.2. Calcutta: Indian Studies: Past & Present. (First published 1880).

Mukherjee, P., 1940, *The History of Medieval Vaisnavism in Orissa*, Calcutta: R. Chatterjee.

——, 1977, *The History of the Jagannath Temple in the 19th century*, Calcutta: Firma K.L. Mukhopadhyay.

Monier-Williams, Sir Monier, 1976, *A Sanskrit-English Dictionary*, Delhi: Motilal Banarsidass, (First published 1899).

O'Malley, L.S.S. 1908, *Puri, Bengal District Gazetteers*, Calcutta.

——, 1913, *Census of India* 1911, Vol 5, Bihar and orissa, Part III, Tables, Calcutta.

——, 1929, *Puri (Bihar and Orissa District Gazetteers).* Revised edition by P.T. Mansfield, Patna: Superintendent, Government Printing Press.

——, 1974, *Indian Caste Customs*, Delhi: Vikas Publishing House. (First published, 1932).

Padhi, B.M., 1975, *Daru Devata*, Cuttack: Cuttack Students' Stores, (First Published 1964). Oriya.

Panigrahi, K.C., 1958-60, "Battle of Devarakonda as described in a story of the Oriya Mahabharata", in: *Journal Andhra Historical Research Society*, Vol. 25, pp. 19-27.

——, 1961, *Chronology of the Bhauma-Karas and the Soma-vamsis of Orissa.*

——, 1963, *Itihasa O'Kimbadanti*, Bhubaneswar: Utkal University. Oriya.

——, 1975, *Sarala Dasa*, New Delhi: Sahitya Akademi.

——, 1976, *Sarala Sahityara Aiyihasika Citra*, Cuttack: Prajatantra Pracar Samiti Oriya.

——, 1981, *History of Orissa (Hindu Period)*, Cuttack: Kitab Mahal.

Ramamurti, G.V., 1938, *The Sora-English Dictionary*, Madras: Government of Madras.

Risley, H.H. 1981, The Tribes and castes of Bengal. (First published 1891).

Rosel, Jakob, 1980, *Der Palast des Herrn der Welt*, Munchen, London: Weltforum Verlag.

Russell, R.V. and Lal, Rai Bahadur Hira, 1975, *The Tribes and Castes of the Central Provinces of India*, Vol. 4, Delhi: Rajdhani Book Centre, (First published 1916).

Sahu, N.K. (ed.) 1956a, *A History of Orissa*, Vol. 1. Calcutta: Susil Gupta (India) Ltd.

——, 1956b, *A History of Orissa*, Vol.2. Calcutta: Susil Gupta (India) Ltd.

Shah, A.M., 1974, "Historical Sociology, A Trend Report", in: *A Survey of Research in Sociology and Social Anthropology*, Vol. 1, pp. 432-59, Bombay: Popular Prakashan.

Silverberg, J. (ed.) 1968, *Social Mobility in the Caste System in India*, The Hague: Mouton.

Singer, Milton, 1972, *When a Great Tradition Modernizes*, New York: Praeger Publishers.

Singh, Jagabandhu, 1964, *Pracina Utkala*, Bhubaneswar: Orissa Sahitya Akademi, (First Published 1929).

Singh, Yogendra, 1974, "Concepts and Theories of Social Change. A Trend Report", in: *A Survey of Research in Sociology and Social Anthropology*, Vol. 1, pp. 384-431, Bombay: Popular Prakashan.

Sinha, Surajit, 1962, "State Formation and Rajput Myth in Tribal Central India", in: *Man in India*, 42/1, pp. 35-80.

——, 1974, "Sociology of Religion, A Trend Report", in: *A Survey of Research in Sociology and Social Anthropology*, Vol. 2, pp. 508-30, Bombay: Popular Prakashan.

Sircar, D.C., 1949/50, "Nagari Plates of Anangabhima III, Saka 1151 and 1152", in: *Epigraphia Indica*, Vol. 28, Part V and VI, pp. 235-58.

Sircar, D.C. and Ratha Sarma, Sadasiva, 1955/56, "Dasagoba Plates of Rajaraja III, Saka 1120", in: *Epigraphia Indica*, Vol. 31, pp. 249-63.

Sontheimer, Guenther-Dietz, 1987," The Vana and the Ksetra: The Tribal Background of some famous Cults", in: *Religion and Society in Eastern India. Eschmann Memorial Lectures* Vol. 1, by G.C. Tripathi, Hermann Kulke (eds.) 1987, pp. 117-64. Bhubaneswar: Eschmann Memorial Fund.

Srinivas, M.N., 1965, *Religion and Society among the Coorgs of South India*, (reprint).

, 1984, Soc*ial Change in Modern India*, New Delhi: Orient Longman Ltd., (First Published 1966).

Stein, Burton, 1968, "Social Mobility and Medieval South Indian Hindu Sects", in: *Social Mobility in the Caste Systems in India*, by J. Silverberg (ed.) 1968, pp. 78-94, The Hague: Mouton.

Stietencron, H. von., 1977," The Date of the Jagannatha Temple: Literary Sources Reconsidered", in *Side Lights on History and Culture of Orissa*, by M.N. Das (ed.) 1977 pp. 516-32, Cuttack: Vidyapuri.

———, 1978a," The Advent of Vaisnavism in Orissa: An Outline of its History according to Archaeological and Epigraphical Sources from the Gupta Period up to 1135 AD", in: *The Cult of Jagannatha and the Regional Tradition of Orissa*, by A. Eschmann, H. Kulke and G.C. Tripathi (eds.) 1978, pp. 1-30.

———, 1978b, "Early Temples of Jagannatha in Orissa: The Forative Phase", in: *The Cult of Jagannatha and the Regional Tradition of Orissa*, by A. Eschmann, H. Kulke and G.C. Tripathi (eds.) 1978, pp. 61-78.

Swain, S.K., 1989, *A Portrait of Population, Orissa (Census of India 1981)*, New Delhi: The Controller of Publications.

Thruston, E., 1975, *The Caste and Tribe of South India*, Vol. 6, Delhi: Cosmo Publications, (First published 1909).

Tripathi, B., 1973, *A Portrait of Population, Orissa*, (*Census of India 1971*), New Delhi: The Controller of Publications.

Tripathi, G.C., 1978, "Navakalevara: The Unique Ceremony of the 'birth' and the 'death' of the Lord of the World", in: *The Cult of Jagannatha and the Regional Tradition of Orissa*, by A. Eschmann, H. Kulke and G.C. Tripathi (eds.) 1978, pp. 223-64.

Vansina, Jan, 1965, *Oral Tradition: A Study in Historical Methodology*, Chicago: Aldine Publishing Company.

Vidyarthi, L.P., 1969, "Studies on Social Change in Tribal India: A Methodological Review", in: *Conflict Tension and Cultural Trend in India*, by L.P. Vidyarthi (ed.) Calcutta: Punthi Pustak.

Vidyarthi, L.P. and Rai, B.K., 1977, *The Tribal Culture of India*, Delhi: Concept Publishing Company.